Everyone's First Cookbook

EVERYONE'S

FIRST

COOKBOOK

MUD PUDDLE BOOKS, INC.
NEW YORK

EVERYONE'S FIRST COOKBOOK

Copyright © 2005

By Sheryn R. Jones

Published by

Mud Puddle Books, Inc.

54 West 21st Street

Suite 601

New York, New York 10010

info@mudpuddlebooks.com

ISBN: 1-59412-066-8

Portions of this book have previously appeared in Easy Comfort Food, Easy Classic Desserts and The Ultimate Cooking with 4-Ingredients.

Printed in China

Original design by Elizabeth Elsas

Table of Contents

DELICIOUS DINNERS

DELECTABLE DESSERTS

PERFECT PIES

CLASSIC CAKES

PUDDINGS, COBBLERS & ICE CREAMS

COOKIES, BROWNIES & FUDGE

INTRODUCTION

Everyone's First Cookbook makes life better!

Life just feels better when we sit down at the dinner table with family and friends to eat food that everybody enjoys. How do you feel when you see Mom's special spaghetti sauce and meatballs or maybe meatloaf with macaroni and cheese and chocolate chip cookies for dessert? Maybe you have special memories of fried chicken, cream gravy, mashed potatoes, green bean casserole and lemon meringue pie for dessert. *Everyone's First Cookbook* captures the classic recipes everyone loves and makes them easy to prepare.

If you don't cook much, lose your fear! *Everyone's First Cookbook* is easy! You'll find a great variety of all your family favorites here and you will love how it feels to have prepared great home-cooked meals featuring all your favorite foods.

Even if you're a frequent cook, you may have forgotten some of the classic recipes that you grew up with. Or, maybe you think everybody's tired of them. Think again. Read this cookbook. You will not be able to resist making these recipes and you'll be glad you did.

Turn your kitchen table into the dinner table. Move the packages, projects and papers scattered on top of the table and move in the people, food and the warmth and comfort of those around you.

Everyone's First Cookbook is loaded with recipes passed from grandmothers to their daughters and then again to their daughters' daughters. These are the tried-and-true recipes, our favorites and the foods that we remember from our childhood.

Food brings us together and provides the foundation to build our memories. You're never too young to cook or too old to stop. Food memories are for all of us.

Enjoy these great, classic recipes.

U.S. MEASUREMENT AND METRIC CONVERSION CHART

Here is a simple chart that makes conversion from U.S. measurements to metric as easy as pie.

1 TEASPOON	5 ML
2 TEASPOONS	10 ML
1 TABLESPOON	15 ML
2 TABLESPOONS	30 ML
1 CUP	237 ML
2 CUPS = 1 PINT	473 ML
3 CUPS	710 ML
4 CUPS = 1 QUART	.95 LITER
4 QUARTS = 1 GALLON	3.8 LITERS
1 OUNCE	28 GRAMS
2 OUNCES	57 GRAMS
3 OUNCES	85 GRAMS
4 OUNCES	113 GRAMS
6 OUNCES	170 GRAMS
8 OUNCES	227 GRAMS
16 OUNCES = 1 POUND	454 GRAMS
2.2 POUNDS	1 KILOGRAM

U.S. MEASUREMENT TO METRIC CONVERSION FORMULAS

TO CONVERT:	MULTIPLY WHAT YOU KNOW BY:
CUPS TO LITERS	x .236
CUPS TO MILLILITERS	x 236.6
GALLONS TO LITERS	x 3.8
OUNCES (FLUID) TO MILLILITERS	x 29.6
OUNCES (WEIGHT) TO GRAMS	x 28.4
PINTS TO LITERS	x .47
POUNDS TO KILOGRAMS	x .45
QUARTS TO LITERS	x .95
TABLESPOONS TO MILLILITERS	x 14.8
TEASPOONS TO MILLILITERS	x 4.9

Everyone's First Cookbook

BREAKFAST FAVORITES

♨ WESTERN OMELETTE

6 eggs

6 tablespoons milk

½ cup grated cheddar cheese

½ cup diced cooked ham

¼ cup finely chopped onion

*¼ cup finely chopped green peppers
   or chopped green chilies, drained*

¼ cup chopped tomatoes

Salsa

Beat eggs with milk. Over medium heat melt butter in omelette pan or skillet and pour one half the eggs into pan. Tilt pan or use spoon to move liquid of eggs around pan to cook evenly. Cook until eggs are almost firm in the middle. Sprinkle cheese, ham, onion, green peppers and tomatoes over one half the eggs. Fold other half of omelette over to cover cheese mixture and continue cooking 1 or 2 minutes longer or until eggs are firm and cheese melts. Slide out of pan, pour salsa over top and serve immediately.

♨ BACON-CHEESE OMELETTE

2 strips bacon

2 eggs

1 tablespoon milk

2 green onions with tops, chopped

1 tablespoon butter

½ cup grated cheddar cheese

Fry bacon crispy, drain, cool and crumble. Sauté onion in remaining bacon drippings and drain. Beat eggs with milk. Over medium heat melt butter in omelette pan and pour in egg mixture. Tilt pan or use spoon to move liquid of eggs around pan to cook evenly. Cook until eggs are almost firm in center. Sprinkle bacon, onions and cheese evenly over half of eggs. Fold one half of omelette over to cover cheese and continue cooking 1 or 2 minutes until cheese melts. Serve immediately.

FRENCH TOAST

2 eggs
1 cup milk
1 tablespoon sugar
1 teaspoon vanilla or ground cinnamon
1 tablespoon butter
6 to 8 slices white bread
Powdered sugar
Maple syrup

Beat eggs, milk, sugar and vanilla or ground cinnamon. Heat griddle until butter melts. Dip both sides of bread into milk-egg mixture. Cook on both sides until brown. Remove from griddle and sprinkle with powdered sugar or maple syrup.

CRISPY FRENCH TOAST:

Crispy French Toast has a crust or coating on outside that makes it crispy. Use ½ cup flour in batter to make crust. Cook until crispy.

Note: Many kinds of breads may be used for French Toast. Possibilities include Texas toast about one-inch thick, challah or French bread cut in thick slices.

BASIC PANCAKES

2 cups flour
1 tablespoon sugar
1 tablespoon baking powder
¼ teaspoon salt
2 eggs
1½ to 2 cups milk, divided
Vegetable oil
Maple syrup
½ cup melted butter

Combine flour, sugar, baking powder and salt in large mixing bowl. In separate bowl, beat eggs and 1½ cups milk. Pour egg mixture into flour mixture and stir until smooth. If batter is too thick, add a little milk. (There will be a few lumps in batter.) Heat griddle and coat lightly with oil. Slowly pour circle of batter on griddle to equal desired size of pancake. After bubbles form on top and edges brown, gently flip pancake to cook other side. Serve immediately with warm syrup and melted butter.

BLUEBERRY PANCAKES:

Wash and drain thoroughly about 1 cup fresh or frozen blueberries. (If blueberries are frozen, do not thaw before adding to pancake batter.) Stir into pancake batter gently and pour onto griddle or skillet.

BUTTERMILK PANCAKES:

Substitute buttermilk instead of milk. If batter is too thick, add just a little milk.

BANANA PANCAKES:

Slice 1 or 2 ripe bananas about ¼-inch thick. When batter is poured onto griddle, place as many slices as desired on batter and lightly push bananas into batter. Cook slowly to make sure inside is firm.

Note: Other variations include apples, cranberries, coconut, bacon, ham and pecans.

BUTTERMILK WAFFLES

2 eggs, separated

2 tablespoons oil

2 cups (1 pint) buttermilk

2¼ cups flour

1½ teaspoons baking powder

½ teaspoon baking soda

½ teaspoon salt

Beat egg yolks with oil and add buttermilk. Combine dry ingredients and add to buttermilk mixture. In separate bowl beat egg whites until stiff peaks form. Slowly fold into batter. Bake in preheated sprayed waffle iron until crispy brown.

CRISPY WAFFLES

2 cups biscuit mix

1 egg

½ cup oil

1⅓ cups club soda

Preheat waffle iron. Combine biscuit mix, egg, oil and club soda in mixing bowl and stir by hand until well blended. Pour just enough batter to cover waffle iron and cook about 5 to 7 minutes until golden brown.

Tip: To make buttermilk, mix 1 cup milk with 1 tablespoon lemon juice or vinegar and set aside for 10 minutes before using.

BISCUITS AND SAUSAGE GRAVY

3 cups biscuit mix

¾ cup milk

½ pound ground, pork sausage

¼ cup (½ stick) butter

⅓ cup flour

3¼ cups milk

½ teaspoon salt

½ teaspoon pepper

Preheat oven to 400°. To make biscuits combine biscuit mix and milk in medium bowl and stir to mix. Put wax paper on counter top and sprinkle lightly with flour. Roll out dough to ¾-inch thick and cut out circles with floured cookie cutter or drinking glass. Put on sprayed baking sheet and bake for 12 to 15 minutes or until golden brown. Cook sausage in skillet and drain drippings except for about 1 to 2 tablespoons. Add butter to drippings and melt. Add flour and cook 1 minute, stirring constantly. Gradually add milk and cook over medium heat, stirring constantly, until gravy thickens. Stir in seasonings and crumbled sausage or serve sausage on the side. Serve gravy immediately and pour over biscuits.

LUSCIOUS
LUNCHES

OLD-FASHIONED TOMATO SOUP

2½ pounds fresh tomatoes, peeled,
seeded, chopped or 4 cups canned
stewed, chopped tomatoes
3 to 4 cups chicken stock
2 ribs celery, minced
1 carrot, minced
1 onion, minced
2 tablespoons basil
Salt
Pepper
Lemon juice

In large soup pot, combine tomatoes, chicken stock, celery, carrot, onion and basil on high heat. After soup begins to boil, reduce heat to low and simmer for 15 to 30 minutes. Add basil, salt and pepper to taste. Use fresh lemon juice, a little at a time, and taste.

CREAM OF TOMATO SOUP:

Omit chicken stock and onion and substitute 2 to 3 cups half-and-half cream. Bring to almost boiling and reduce heat to simmer.

CHICKEN-NOODLE SOUP

Chicken stock
1 (3-4 pound) whole chicken
1 carrot, chopped
2 ribs celery with leaves, chopped
½ to ¾ cup egg noodles, cooked
Salt
Pepper

Wash whole chicken and giblets and put in large soup pot. Add 7 to 8 cups water, carrot and celery and bring to boil. Reduce heat and simmer, partially covered, for 30 minutes to 1 hour or until meat is tender. Remove chicken from soup pot and cool. Continue simmering and spoon off fat from top of liquid when needed. Bone chicken and put all bones and skin back into soup pot. Continue to simmer for 3 to 4 hours. Turn heat off and strain chicken stock in large bowl. Add chopped chicken and cooked egg noodles. Salt and pepper to taste.

CHICKEN SOUP WITH RICE:

Omit noodles and add 1½ tablespoons uncooked rice to chicken stock. Cook until rice is done.

 EASY CAESAR SALAD

1 (1.2 ounce) package Caesar salad dressing
½ head romaine lettuce
¼ cup shredded parmesan cheese
Croutons

Tear lettuce in small pieces. Pour on Caesar salad dressing and toss. Add shredded parmesan cheese and croutons. Chill before serving.

COBB SALAD

2 to 3 boneless, skinless chicken breast halves
6 slices bacon
½ head iceberg lettuce
½ head romaine lettuce
1 avocado, peeled, pitted, diced
3 hard-boiled eggs, diced
2 green onions with tops, chopped
2 tomatoes, peeled, diced
¾ cup shredded, sharp cheddar cheese
1 ounce crumbled roquefort cheese
Salad dressing of choice

In large saucepan boil chicken breast halves in enough water to cover for 30 to 40 minutes. Cool and dice. Fry bacon crispy, drain, cool and crumble. Tear iceberg and romaine lettuce in small pieces and toss together in salad bowl. Arrange each ingredient in its own area on top of lettuce: one area for chicken, one for bacon, one for avocado, one for eggs, one for onion and one for tomatoes. Sprinkle with both cheeses or arrange them in their own areas. Chill before serving. Serve with favorite dressing.

TUNA FISH SALAD

1 (12 ounce) can tuna fish, drained
½ cup chopped celery
¼ cup chopped pecans
2 hard-boiled eggs, finely chopped
¼ teaspoon onion salt
Mayonnaise

Drain tuna and put in medium bowl. Add celery, pecans, eggs, onion salt and enough mayonnaise to moisten mixture. Chill and serve.

CHICKEN SALAD

6 to 8 boneless, skinless chicken breast halves
½ cup chopped celery
½ cup chopped onion
2 hard-boiled eggs, diced
6 tablespoons mayonnaise
Salt & Pepper

In large saucepan boil chicken breast halves in enough water to cover for 30 to 40 minutes. Cool, dice chicken and place in large bowl. Add onion, celery, eggs and mayonnaise and mix well. Salt and pepper to taste. Spread on favorite bread, mound on lettuce leaves or stuff in hollowed out tomato.

EGG SALAD

4 hard-boiled eggs
⅓ cup mayonnaise
1 tablespoon Dijon mustard
1 rib celery, minced or chopped
Salt & Pepper

Mash eggs with fork and stir in mayonnaise, mustard and celery. Add salt and pepper to taste. Spread on bread and serve as sandwiches.

♘ GRILLED CHEESE SANDWICHES

Butter

Bread

American, cheddar or processed cheese slices

Butter 1 side of bread slice and put in hot skillet over medium-high heat. Add cheese over bread and put another bread slice, buttered on 1 side, on top. Cook 2 to 3 minutes for cheese to melt and bread to brown. Flatten sandwich slightly with spatula. If bread slices stick together, turn sandwich with spatula and brown other side. When second side is brown, serve immediately.

Note: Add some of the following ingredients for a change: ham slice, lunch meat slice, cooked, crispy slices of bacon, thin slices of tomato, jalapenos, thin slices of onion, mozzarella cheese, parmesan cheese, sharp cheddar cheese, Monterey Jack cheese and Swiss cheese.

POTATO SALAD

6 large potatoes
1 hard-boiled egg, chopped
1 medium onion, chopped
½ bell pepper, chopped
2 ribs celery, chopped
¼ cup sweet pickle relish, drained
1 large dill pickle, chopped
Salt & Pepper
1½ teaspoons mustard
½ cup mayonnaise

Peel and wash potatoes, cut each potato in 4 to 6 pieces and put in large saucepan. Cover with water and boil until potatoes are tender. Cool and cut potatoes into bite-size pieces. Stir together cubed potatoes, egg, onion, bell pepper, celery, pickle relish, dill pickle, salt, pepper, mustard and mayonnaise and mix well. Chill and serve.

COLE SLAW

½ cup mayonnaise
1 teaspoon vinegar
⅛ teaspoon salt
⅛ teaspoon white pepper
⅛ teaspoon sugar
Dash Worcestershire sauce
1 small head cabbage
1 small carrot, shredded
½ bell pepper, sliced thinly

Mix mayonnaise, vinegar, salt, white pepper, sugar and Worcestershire sauce in small bowl and set aside. (It may be necessary to double these to cover cabbage.) Shred or slice cabbage into very thin slices and put in medium bowl. Add carrot and bell pepper and toss. Add mayonnaise mixture to cabbage and toss until cabbage is coated with dressing.

DELICIOUS DINNERS

꩜ Spaghetti and Meatballs

Meatballs:

2 pounds lean ground round

½ pound ground pork

4 eggs

2 cups grated Italian cheese

1½ cups dry French breadcrumbs, rolled fine

1 onion, chopped

2 cloves garlic, pressed

½ bunch fresh parsley, minced

½ cup milk

1½ tablespoons ketchup

Salt & Pepper

Olive oil

Toss all ingredients lightly and shape into balls. Brown in olive oil and set aside.

Sauce:

1 onion, minced

1 clove garlic, pressed

1 tablespoon olive oil

2 (6 ounce) cans tomato paste

1½ to 2 quarts water

Salt & Pepper

1 tablespoon minced sweet basil

1 tablespoon ground oregano

In heavy saucepan sauté onion and garlic in olive oil until soft and clear. Add tomato paste, water, salt, pepper, basil and oregano and mix well. Add browned meat balls and simmer for 1 hour or until sauce thickens. Serve over cooked spaghetti. Serves 6 to 8.

Pot Roast

1 (4 to 5 pound) boneless rump roast
Seasoned salt
Seasoned pepper
Garlic powder
2 cups water
6 medium potatoes, peeled, quartered
8 carrots, peeled, quartered
3 onions, peeled, quartered

Preheat oven to 375º. Place roast in roasting pan with lid and sprinkle liberally with salt, pepper and garlic powder. Add 2 cups water and bake covered for about 30 minutes. Lower heat to 325º and bake covered for 3 hours. Add potatoes, carrots and onions. Bake another 35 to 40 minutes. Lift roast from pan and place on serving dish. Arrange potatoes, carrots and onion around roast.

GRAVY:

3 tablespoons cornstarch
¾ cup water
½ teaspoon pepper
½ teaspoon salt

Combine cornstarch and water and pour into juices in roaster. Add pepper and salt. On stove burner, cook juices on high and stir constantly until gravy thickens. Serve in gravy boat with roast and vegetables. Serves 8.

☙ MEATLOAF

1½ pounds ground round

1 teaspoon salt

1 egg

½ cup milk

1 cup crushed breadcrumbs

½ cup chopped onion

1 (6 ounce) can tomato paste

Preheat oven to 325º. In large bowl mix ground round, salt, egg, milk, breadcrumbs, onion and tomato paste. Form meat mixture to loaf. Place in sprayed 9 x 9- inch baking dish. Bake 50 to 60 minutes.

Variations:

Add ½ cup grated cheese to meat mixture.

Instead of using all ground round, use half ground round and half ground pork.

Add slice of bacon on top before cooking.

Add tomato sauce.

TOMATO SAUCE:

2 tablespoons olive oil

¾ cup tomato paste

2½ cups canned, chopped stewed tomatoes

1 teaspoon sugar

5 tablespoons butter

Salt

Pepper

In heavy saucepan over medium heat, heat oil and stir in tomato paste, stewed tomatoes, sugar and butter. Simmer for about 30 minutes. Add salt and pepper to taste. Pour over meatloaf during last 15 minutes of cooking or serve on the side.

♈ TURKEY AND DRESSING OR STUFFING

1 (15 to 18 pound) turkey

1 cup butter, softened

Salt

Pepper

1–2 ribs celery, quartered

1 white onion, peeled

Put turkey in refrigerator to thaw 3 to 4 days before cooking. When ready to cook, remove metal clamp from legs. Run cold water into breast and neck cavities until giblets and neck can be removed. (Interior should be cold to slightly icy.) Refrigerate until ready to cook.

To cook turkey, preheat oven to 325°. Rub entire turkey with butter and lightly salt and pepper. Place turkey in roaster, breast side up. Cover bottom of pan with ½ to 1 cup water. Place 1 or 2 ribs celery and ½ peeled white onion inside the cavity. Cover with lid or foil. Follow cooking time chart and baste occasionally with drippings while turkey is cooking.

COOKING TIMES FOR TURKEY:

Weight of turkey	Cooking time at 325°
6 to 8 pounds	*3 to 3½ hours*
8 to 12 pounds	*3½ to 4½ hours*
12 to 16 pounds	*4½ to 5½ hours*
16 to 20 pounds	*5½ to 6½ hours*
20 to 24 pounds	*6½ to 7 hours*

DRESSING OR STUFFING:

The same recipe can work for dressing or stuffing. Dressing is usually a side dish prepared in a baking dish and stuffing is put inside the cavity of the bird. Both are great and tradition usually determines how it is served.

2 (7.5 ounce) boxes cornbread mix

9 biscuits

1 small onion, chopped

2 ribs celery, chopped

2 eggs

Pepper

2 teaspoons poultry seasoning

3 (14 ounce) cans chicken broth, divided

Before making dressing, prepare cornbread and biscuits according to package directions. Preheat oven to 350°. Crumble cornbread and biscuits into large bowl using a little more cornbread than biscuits. Add onion, celery, eggs and seasonings. Stir in 2½ cans chicken broth. If mixture is not "runny", add rest of broth. (If it is still not runny, add a little milk.) Bake in sprayed 9 x 13-inch glass baking dish at 350° for about 45 minutes or until golden brown. (This may be frozen uncooked and thawed just before cooking.)

GRAVY:

2 (10 ounce) cans chicken broth, divided

2 heaping tablespoons cornstarch

Giblets from turkey

Salt

Pepper

2 hard-boiled eggs, sliced

To make gravy, mix cornstarch with ½ cup chicken broth and stir until there are no lumps. Add remaining broth, giblets, salt and pepper and cook on medium for about 1 hour, stirring frequently, until giblets are done and broth thickens. Remove giblets, chop finely and put back in gravy. Add boiled eggs, pour in gravy boat and serve.

❧ GOULASH

1 cup uncooked macaroni

1½ pounds ground chuck

5 tablespoons chili powder

1 (15 ounce) can tomato sauce

1 cup shredded colby cheese

In medium saucepan bring 3 cups water to rapid boil. Slowly add macaroni and cook on low until tender. In large skillet brown ground chuck and drain. Add chili powder, tomato sauce and cooked macaroni to meat in skillet. Simmer on low heat for 30 minutes. Garnish with shredded cheese. Add more chili powder if you prefer zestier flavor.

❧ CHICKEN POT PIE

6 to 8 skinless, boneless chicken breast halves

¼ cup (½ stick) butter

2¼ cups biscuit mix, divided

1½ teaspoons salt

½ teaspoon pepper

2 (10 ounce) cans chicken stock, divided

⅔ cup whipping cream or half-and-half

½ cup milk

Note: If you want to do this like grandmother made it, bake a whole chicken and strain juices to make chicken stock. Of course, you will need to make biscuits from scratch, too.

Bake or boil chicken breasts until tender, cool and cut into pieces. Preheat oven to 350°. In small saucepan melt butter and stir in ¼ cup biscuit mix, salt and pepper. Remove from heat and stir in all but 3 tablespoons chicken stock, cream and chicken. Cook over low heat about 5 minutes until mixture thickens. In separate bowl mix remaining 2 cups biscuit mix, remaining 3 tablespoons chicken stock and milk vigorously with fork. Spread wax paper on counter and sprinkle with flour. Knead dough 8 to 10 times on wax paper. Pat or roll dough to fit top of 4 to 5 individual baking dishes or 9 x 9-inch baking pan. Pour hot filling into baking dish, cover with dough and bake about 15 minutes or until top is golden brown.

♆ GRILLED PORK CHOPS

4 (1 inch) thick center-cut pork chops
2 to 3 tablespoons olive oil
2 tablespoons fresh lemon juice
Salt
Pepper
1 lemon

Start charcoal fire or heat gas grill. Allow pork chops to reach room temperature. When fire is ready, dry pork chops with paper towel and season with olive oil, a little lemon juice and a lot of salt and pepper. Place pork chops on grill and sear both sides for a minute or two to seal the juices inside. Move to cooler part of grill and cook 5 to 10 minutes or until chops are firm to the touch and juices are slightly pink on the inside. (Cooking time will vary with type of fire, thickness of chops and covered and uncovered grill. The main thing is not to overcook which dries out pork chops.) Remove chops from grill, drizzle with a little more lemon juice and serve immediately.

♆ MACARONI AND CHEESE

1 cup uncooked macaroni, divided
¼ cup (½ stick) butter, sliced
1½ cups grated sharp cheddar,
   Colby or processed cheese
⅔ cup milk
Salt
Pepper
Tabasco, optional

Cook and drain macaroni. Stir in butter and mix to melt butter. Put half macaroni in sprayed, casserole dish. Mix cheese, milk and seasonings and pour half over macaroni. Pour remaining macaroni into dish and cover with remaining cheese mixture. Bake at 350° until light brown on top.

 FRIED CHICKEN

1 chicken, cut up or 10 to 12 chicken pieces

Salt

Pepper

2 tablespoons cream, milk or buttermilk

2 eggs, beaten

Flour

Oil

Rinse and pat dry each piece of chicken and place on wax paper. Salt and pepper each piece of chicken on both sides. Add cream or milk to beaten eggs and dip chicken in egg mixture. Roll in flour to coat all sides. Heat ¼ inch oil in heavy skillet. Brown chicken on both sides. Lower heat and cook until tender, about 25 minutes. When done, remove chicken and drain on paper towels.

Tip: For a thicker batter, dip chicken in egg mixture and flour several times.

GRAVY:

3 tablespoons flour

½ teaspoon salt

½ teaspoon pepper

1½ cups milk

After all chicken fries, add 3 tablespoons flour, salt and pepper to pan drippings. Stir and turn burner to medium heat. Pour in milk and cook, stirring constantly, until gravy thickens.

Tip: To make buttermilk, mix 1 cup milk and 1 tablespoon lemon juice or vinegar and set aside for 10 minutes before using.

CHILI

2 pounds beef chuck, cubed

2 tablespoons oil

1 onion, chopped

3 cloves garlic, chopped

1 (8 ounce) can tomato sauce

1 cup beef broth

3–5 tablespoons chili powder

2 teaspoons ground cumin

½ teaspoon salt

½ teaspoon pepper

Brown beef in hot oil in large, heavy saucepan. Stir in onion, garlic, tomato sauce and beef broth. Stir in 1 tomato sauce can of water and mix well. Add chili powder, cumin, salt and pepper and stir to mix. Cover and simmer for 1 to 2 hours and stir occasionally. If liquid is too thin, remove cover and continue simmering.

Note: To make chili hotter, add more chili powder or slices of seeded jalapenos. Add additional seasonings a little at a time, cook 10 minutes and taste. Of course, you can use ground beef instead of chuck roast, but "chili heads" would not approve.

BAKED BEANS

1 (1 pound) can pork and beans

4 tablespoons brown sugar

¼ teaspoon dry mustard

¼ cup ketchup

¼ cup chopped green pepper

¼ cup chopped onion

3 or 4 slices bacon, halved

Preheat oven to 350°. Combine beans, sugar, ketchup, onion, green pepper and mustard and mix well. Pour into sprayed, casserole dish and top with bacon. Bake for 1 hour. Serve immediately.

❧ Barbecued Ribs

There are as many dry rubs and barbecue sauces as there are cooks. Here are three from which to choose.

Ribs:

8 to 10 pounds spareribs, baby back ribs or country-style ribs

Season ribs with choice of dry rubs or sauces as directed below and on next page. Grill ribs over medium hot charcoal or gas fire until ribs are tender or for 1 to 2 hours. (Times vary with size of ribs and heat of fire.) If you want to cook ribs in the oven, roast them for 3 to 4 hours at 275° to 300° in covered roasting pan. Add water if needed. Cook until meat begins to fall off the bones.

Dry Seasoning Rub:

4 tablespoons paprika
2 tablespoons chili powder
1 tablespoon dry mustard
1 teaspoon basil, minced
1 tablespoon meat tenderizer
½ teaspoon cayenne pepper
½ teaspoon onion salt
½ teaspoon garlic salt

Combine all ingredients in medium bowl and mix thoroughly. Rub onto half of ribs and let sit for 1 hour before cooking. Use one of the sauces that follow for the other half of ribs or use dry rub for the entire rack. (Ribs seasoned with a dry rub are considered "dry" and those with barbecue sauces are said to be "wet".)

Barbecue Sauce:

1 cup chopped onion

½ cup oil

1 cup ketchup

⅓ cup fresh lemon juice

3 tablespoons sugar

3 tablespoons Worcestershire sauce

2 tablespoons prepared mustard

2 teaspoons salt

1 teaspoon pepper

Sauté onion in oil until soft and clear. Add remaining ingredients. Simmer for 30 minutes. Use sauce on ribs during the last hour of cooking. The sugar in the sauce will burn if you apply it before the last hour of cooking. Sauce makes about 3 cups.

Teriyaki Sauce:

¼ cup teriyaki sauce or soy sauce

¼ cup white wine

1 clove garlic, minced

2 tablespoons brown sugar

2 tablespoons Worcestershire sauce

Combine all ingredients. Marinate meat or vegetables. Baste while cooking.

♆ BARBECUED BRISKET

1 (7 pound) trimmed beef brisket
1 (4 ounce) bottle liquid smoke
½ teaspoon garlic salt
½ teaspoon onion salt
½ teaspoon celery salt
1 teaspoon seasoned pepper

Preheat oven to 350º. Place brisket in large baking pan and coat generously with liquid smoke. Sprinkle spices over brisket and cover pan with foil or lid. Place in refrigerator overnight. When ready to bake, drain about ¾ of liquid smoke from pan.

SAUCE:

1 (16 ounce) bottle ketchup
½ cup packed brown sugar
1 teaspoon prepared mustard
1½ teaspoons garlic powder
1 tablespoons Worcestershire sauce
⅛ teaspoon cayenne pepper
¼ cup vinegar

Combine ketchup, brown sugar, mustard, garlic powder, worcestershire, cayenne pepper and vinegar in saucepan and blend well. Cook over medium heat until mixture thickens. Pour over brisket and cook at 350º for 1 hour. Lower heat to 275º and cook for 4 to 5 hours.

✒ MASHED POTATOES

3 to 4 large russet potatoes
¼ cup milk
⅓ cup butter
1 teaspoon salt
1 teaspoon white pepper

Variation: Add 1 teaspoon garlic salt.

Peel, cut each potato into 4 to 6 pieces and boil in enough water to cover in medium saucepan until tender. Drain water and pour potatoes into mixing bowl. Cool and cut into small pieces. In mixing bowl, beat potatoes until they are well blended, but still lumpy. Add milk, butter, salt and pepper. Whip potatoes until smooth and creamy.

Tip: White pepper does not leave black specs in potatoes like black pepper does.

✒ CREAMY MASHED POTATOES

6 large potatoes
1 (8 ounce) carton sour cream
1 (8 ounce) package cream cheese, softened
1 teaspoon salt
½ teaspoon white pepper

Preheat oven to 325º. Peel, cut up and boil potatoes until tender. Drain water and whip hot potatoes with sour cream, cream cheese, salt and pepper. Whip until cream cheese melts. Pour in greased 3-quart baking dish. Cover with foil and bake for 20 minutes. Serves 8 to 10.

♧ BROILED STEAK

1 (1-2 inch thick) sirloin, porterhouse or
    T-bone steak
Oil
Salt
Fresh ground pepper

Allow steak to come to room temperature. Preheat oven on broil. Lightly oil broiler rack and put in a drip pan. With rack about 4 inches below broiler, cook steak about 3 to 5 minutes on each side for rare and longer for well done. Season with salt and pepper before serving.

♧ GRILLED FILET MIGNON

4 (8 ounce) filets
Salt
Fresh ground black pepper

Preheat charcoal or gas grill and clean grate before cooking. When the flames of charcoal fire have turned into a low fire of red hot coals, put filets on grill. Cook 3 to 5 minutes on each side according to taste. If meat is soft, it is rare. If it is firm, it is well done. Season with salt and ground pepper to taste.

Tip: Charcoal or propane grills give a slightly smoky flavor to the meat. Pan frying in butter sears the outside of the steak to hold in the juices. Start the steak on high heat just to sear the outside, then reduce the heat. Do not overcook.

CHICKEN-FRIED STEAK AND CREAM GRAVY

½ cup milk

1 egg

¾ cup flour

½ teaspoon salt

¼ teaspoon black pepper

1 (1½ pound) round steak, tenderized

Oil

In small bowl, beat milk and egg. In another small flat bowl, mix flour, salt and pepper. Cut tenderized round steak into 4 to 6 pieces. Coat each cutlet with seasoned flour, dip in milk-egg mixture and coat with seasoned flour again. Press flour into steak during last coating. Pour about 1 inch oil into skillet and heat. When oil sizzles, carefully lay each steak in skillet. Cook on each side until golden brown. Drain on paper towel.

CREAM GRAVY:

¼ cup (½ stick) butter

⅓ cup flour

½ teaspoon salt

½ teaspoon pepper

3¼ cups milk

Drain all drippings except 1 tablespoon from skillet. Add butter and seasonings to melt. Over medium heat stir in ¾ cup milk slowly, stirring constantly, until gravy thickens. Cook until heated thoroughly and serve immediately.

French Fries

4 pounds russet potatoes
Salt
Vegetable oil

Cut potatoes into lengths about ¼ x ¼ x 3 inches. Place in large bowl, cover with water and chill in refrigerator for about 2 hours. Pour oil in deep saucepan to depth of 4 inches and warm over medium heat. Drain potatoes and pat dry with paper towels. When oil begins to sizzle, carefully drop a few potatoes at a time in saucepan and cook about 1 to 2 minutes until crisp and golden. Drain on paper towel and sprinkle with salt. Continue cooking in small batches and serve immediately.

French Green Bean Casserole

2 (14.5 ounce) cans French-cut green beans
1 (5 ounce) can water chestnuts
1 (10 ounce) can cream of mushroom soup
2 cups grated sharp cheddar cheese
2 (2.8 ounce) cans French fried onion rings

Drain green beans and water chestnuts. In medium bowl mix green beans and water chestnuts with mushroom soup. Spray 9 x 13 x 2-inch baking dish and pour green bean mixture into dish. Cover with grated cheese and bake at 350º for 15 minutes. Remove from oven and pour French fried onion rings evenly over top of dish. Bake another 15 to 20 minutes until hot throughout and brown on top.

Beef and Noodle Casserole

1½ cups cooked, cubed beef

2 eggs

1 cup sour cream

½ cup grated Swiss cheese

1 onion, chopped

Salt & Pepper

1 (8 ounce) package egg noodles, cooked

Preheat oven to 350°. Use leftover roast and cut in bite-size pieces. In medium bowl, beat eggs slightly and stir in sour cream. Add Swiss cheese, onion, beef and salt and pepper to taste. Butter 2-quart casserole dish and pour cooked noodles evenly over bottom. Pour cheese-beef sauce over noodles and gently toss to mix. Bake about 15 to 30 minutes or until heated throughout.

Variations: Omit leftover beef and substitute 1½ cups cooked, chopped chicken or 1½ cups cooked, chopped ham.

Chicken-Noodle Casserole

1 (6 ounce) package noodles, divided

1 (10 ounce) can cream of chicken soup

1 (5⅓ ounce) can evaporated milk

¼ teaspoon salt

1 cup shredded cheddar cheese

3 cups diced, cooked chicken

1 cup diced celery

¼ cup diced pimiento, drained

1 cup slivered almonds, toasted, divided

Toasted, buttered breadcrumbs

Preheat oven to 400°. Cook noodles according to package directions and drain. Place half noodles in each of 2 small, sprayed casseroles or 1 large casserole dish. Combine soup, milk and salt in medium saucepan and heat, stirring constantly. Add cheese and stir until cheese melts. Add chicken, celery, pimiento and half the almonds and stir to mix well. Pour mixture over noodles in casserole dishes. Bake uncovered for about 20 minutes to heat thoroughly.

FRIED FISH

Fish fillets
Corn meal
Salt
Pepper
Oil

Lay fish fillets on wax paper and pat dry on both sides. Pour corn meal into wide-mouth bowl. Sprinkle salt and pepper in corn meal and mix thoroughly. Dip several fish fillets in corn meal mixture and coat both sides. In heavy skillet pour oil to cover half the fish. Heat oil until it bubbles slightly. Carefully slide each fish fillet into skillet. (Be careful not to splash hot oil.) Brown well and turn once. When second side browns, lift from pan and drain on paper towels. Serve immediately.

TARTAR SAUCE:

½ cup mayonnaise
¼ cup India relish, drained

Mix mayonnaise and relish and serve. Amount of relish may vary according to taste.

COCKTAIL SAUCE:

1½ cups cocktail sauce
4 tablespoons lemon juice
3 tablespoons horseradish
2 teaspoons worcestershire
½ teaspoon grated onion
4 drops hot sauce
Salt to taste

Combine all ingredients and chill for several hours before serving.

Party Pizza

1 pound ground sausage
1 (14 ounce) jar pizza sauce
1½ teaspoons oregano
¼ teaspoon garlic powder
1 cup chopped onion
½ cup shredded parmesan cheese
½ cup grated mozzarella cheese
1 (10 inch) pizza crust

In medium skillet cook and drain sausage and set aside. To pizza sauce, add oregano and garlic powder. Spread pizza sauce evenly over pizza crust. Sprinkle sausage, onion, parmesan cheese and mozzarella cheese on top of pizza sauce. (Add additional ingredients according to your own taste.) Bake at 350° until cheese melts and pizza is bubbly on top.

Variations: Add pepperoni slices, ground beef, Canadian bacon slices, green olives, black olives, bell pepper, mushrooms, jalapenos and/or anchovies.

 Cheeseburger

1 pound bacon

2 pounds ground beef

Salt

Pepper

8 slices cheese

8 hamburger buns

1 large onion, sliced

Lettuce

Tomatoes

Pickle slices

Mustard

Mayonnaise

Ketchup

Fry bacon and drain drippings from pan. Mix ground beef, salt and pepper and form into 8 patties. Cook on charcoal grill or in skillet until almost done. Add cheese slice on top of meat. Allow cheese to melt and put meat on warm bun. Add bacon, onions, lettuce, tomatoes and pickles. Dress with mustard, mayonnaise and/or ketchup.

California Burgers:

Replace ground beef with ground turkey. Use bean sprouts, avocado slices and tomatoes instead of bacon, onions, lettuce and pickles.

Western Burgers:

Replace raw onion with sautéed onion, sautéed fresh mushrooms and add chili sauce, hickory sauce or ketchup.

Southwestern Burgers:

Use green chili salsa and grated Mexican, four-cheese blend.

♆ PINEAPPLE-GLAZED HAM

1 (7 pound) shank or butt-end ham

Whole cloves

1 (14 ounce) can chunk pineapple, drained

Preheat oven to 350º. Stick whole cloves on the outside of ham. With toothpicks stick pineapple chunks on ham.

SAUCE:

1 cup red wine or cooking wine

1 cup packed brown sugar

1 tablespoon cut-up crystallized ginger

1½ teaspoons dijon mustard

1 (8 ounce) can crushed pineapple

In saucepan, combine wine, brown sugar, crystallized ginger, mustard, crushed pineapple and bring to boil. Remove from heat. Place ham in roasting pan and pour hot sauce over ham. Cook for 10 to 15 minutes per pound. Baste with sauce every 20 minutes.

DELECTABLE DESSERTS

PERFECT PIES

CHERRY PIE

4 cups pitted, red tart cherries
1¼ cups sugar
¼ cup flour
¼ teaspoon cinnamon
2 tablespoons butter

Preheat oven to 425°. Prepare crust for 1 (9-inch) pie pan with 2 pie crusts. In large bowl, lightly stir cherries and sugar together. Stir in flour and lemon juice. Spoon into pie pan with bottom crust. Dot with butter and place top crust over pie filling. Fold edges of top crust under edges of bottom crust to seal. Flute edges with fingers. Cut several slits in top crust. Bake for 15 minutes and remove pie from oven. Cover edges of pie crust with foil to keep them from burning. Return to oven and bake for 20 to 25 minutes or until pie is bubbly and crust is golden brown.

APPLE PIE

7 apples, peeled, cored, sliced
½ teaspoon lemon juice
½ cup packed brown sugar
1 (9-inch) double pie crust
¼ cup butter, sliced
1 teaspoon cinnamon
¼ cup sugar

Preheat oven to 400°. In large bowl, combine sliced apples, lemon juice, brown sugar and cinnamon. Pour in prepared pie shell and dollop with butter. Place second pie crust on top of apples and pinch sides to seal. Cut small slits in top pie crust. Sprinkle with sugar. Bake for 30 to 40 minutes or until crust is golden brown.

SOUTHERN APPLE PIE

9-inch partial baked pie crust

¾ cup sugar

2 tablespoons flour

1 cup sour cream

1 egg, beaten

¼ teaspoon salt

½ teaspoon vanilla

2 cups apples, finely chopped

Bake pie crust 7 minutes at 350°.

Increase oven to 450°. Mix sugar, flour, sour cream, egg, salt and vanilla thoroughly, and add apples and mix. Pour in partially baked shell and continue baking for 30 minutes.

TOPPING:

½ cup sugar

6 tablespoons flour

1 teaspoon cinnamon

¼ cup (¼ stick) butter

Blend sugar, flour, cinnamon and butter for topping. Spread on pie and bake and additional 10 minutes. Serves 6 to 8.

4 cups fresh blueberries

¾ cup sugar

¼ cup flour

2 tablespoons lemon juice

2 tablespoons butter

Preheat oven to 425°. Prepare crust for 1 (9-inch) pie pan with 2 pie crusts. In large bowl, lightly stir blueberries and sugar together. (If blueberries are tart, add a little more sugar). Stir in flour and lemon juice. Spoon into pie pan with bottom crust. Dot with butter and place top crust over pie filling. Fold edges of top crust under edges of bottom crust to seal. Flute edges with fingers. Cut several slits in top crust. Bake for 15 minutes and remove pie from oven. Cover edges of pie crust with foil to keep them from burning.

Return to oven and bake at 425° for 30 to 40 minutes or until pie is bubbly and crust is golden brown.

OLD-FASHIONED PEACH PIE

1 (9-inch) double pie shell, unbaked

5 cups peeled, sliced fresh peaches

¾ cup sugar

⅓ cup flour

1 tablespoon lemon juice

2 tablespoons butter

Preheat oven to 425°. Prepare crust for 1 (9-inch) pie pan with 2 pie crusts. In large bowl, lightly stir peaches and sugar together. (If peaches are tart, add a little more sugar.)

Stir in flour and lemon juice. Spoon into pie pan with bottom crust. Dot with butter and place top crust over pie filling. Fold edges of top crust under edges of bottom crust to seal. Flute edges with fingers. Cut several slits in top crust. Bake for 15 minutes and remove pie from oven. Cover edges of pie crust with foil to keep them from burning.

Return to oven and bake for 15 to 20 minutes or until pie is bubbly and crust is light, golden brown.

SNAPPY STRAWBERRY PIE

This 5-minute, easy-to-make pie combines sweet and tart flavors.

1-2 lemons

1 (14 ounce) can sweetened condensed milk

4 ounces frozen whipped topping, thawed

1 (6 ounce) graham cracker crust

1 pint strawberries, hulled, halved

Squeeze lemons to get ¼ cup lemon juice. In medium bowl, combine sweetened condensed milk with lemon juice and whisk until well blended. Gently fold in whipped topping. Pour mixture into prepared pie crust. Arrange strawberry halves in attractive design on top. Keep chilled until ready to serve.

❧ Fresh Strawberry Pie

7 cups fresh strawberries
1¼ cups water
1¼ cups sugar
4 tablespoons cornstarch
1 (9-inch) baked pastry shell

Wash berries and remove hulls. Reserve a few whole berries for garnish. Crush 1 cup of smaller berries, add water and simmer over low heat for 2 minutes. Remove from heat and sieve. Discard pulp. Blend sugar and cornstarch and add to berry juice. Cook slowly, stirring constantly, over low heat until thick and clear. Remove from heat and add a few drops red food coloring. Spread thin coating of glaze on bottom and sides of pastry shell. Divide remaining berries in half and arrange one-half in an even layer on bottom of shell, tips up. Spoon half of glaze over berries carefully coating each one. Repeat, to use remaining berries and glaze. Chill fresh strawberry pie in refrigerator 3 to 4 hours before serving. When ready to serve top as follows.

TOPPING:

1 cup heavy cream
3 tablespoons powdered sugar
1 teaspoon vanilla

Whip cream until stiff peaks form. Gradually add sugar and vanilla and continue whipping until peaks hold very firm. Mound topping on fresh strawberry pie and garnish with reserved berries.

STRAWBERRY-RHUBARB PIE

6 tablespoons flour, divided

1¼ cups sugar, divided

3 cups unpeeled rhubarb, cut in 1-inch pieces

1 cup sliced strawberries

2 tablespoons butter

1 egg white, slightly beaten

¼ cup cinnamon-sugar mixture

1 (9-inch) double pastry shell, unbaked

Preheat oven to 425°. Lightly brush bottom and sides of pastry shell with melted butter and chill. Combine 2 tablespoons flour and 2 tablespoons sugar and sprinkle over chilled pastry. Combine rhubarb and strawberries and pour in pie pan. Combine remaining flour and sugar and sprinkle over rhubarb mixture. Dot with butter. Cut remaining pastry into strips for lattice topping. Brush with egg white. Sprinkle cinnamon-sugar mixture over top of lattice. Bake at 425° for 15 minutes. Lower heat to 350° and bake 40 to 45 minutes longer. Cool 1 hour before serving.

LEMON MERINGUE PIE

1½ cups sugar, divided

3 tablespoons cornstarch

1½ cups cold water

3 egg yolks, slightly beaten

1 lemon, grate rind

¼ cup lemon juice

1 tablespoon butter

1 (9-inch) pie shell, baked

3 egg whites, at room temperature

In 2-quart saucepan, stir 1 cup sugar and cornstarch. Gradually stir in water until smooth. Stir in egg yolks, stirring constantly, bring to boil over medium heat and boil 1 minute. Remove from heat and stir in grated lemon rind, lemon juice and butter. Cool. Pour in pastry shell. In small bowl with mixer at high speed beat egg whites until foamy. Gradually beat in ⅓ cup sugar and continue beating until stiff peaks form. Spoon on top of lemon filling touching crust around edges to seal. Bake at 350° for 15 to 20 minutes or until light brown. Cool before serving.

PUMPKIN PIE

4 slightly beaten eggs

2 cups canned or mashed cooked pumpkin

1 cup sugar

½ cup dark corn syrup

1 teaspoon vanilla

½ teaspoon cinnamon

¼ teaspoon salt

1 (9-inch) pie shell, unbaked

Mix all ingredients and pour into pie shell. Bake at 350° for 40 minutes or until firm in center.

PECAN PIE

2 tablespoons flour

2 tablespoons butter, softened

3 eggs, beaten

⅔ cup sugar

1 cup corn syrup

1 tablespoon vanilla

Pinch salt

1 cup pecans

1 (9-inch) pie shell, unbaked

Preheat oven to 350°. In mixing bowl, blend flour and butter. Add eggs, sugar, corn syrup, vanilla, salt and pecans. Pour in pie crust and bake at 350° for 10 minutes. Reduce heat to 250° and bake 1 hour and 15 minutes.

OLD-FASHIONED PECAN PIE

This vintage recipe is more than 75 years old and was passed down from mothers to daughters.

3 eggs, beaten

1 cup sugar

1 cup white corn syrup

1 cup pecans

1 teaspoon vanilla

1 (9-inch) unbaked pie crust

Preheat oven to 300°. Beat eggs and sugar until lemon colored. Add corn syrup, pecans and vanilla and mix well. Pour into unbaked pie crust. Bake for 1 hour or until center of pie is set.

Frances Parham

BOSTON CREAM PIE

1 (9 ounce) package yellow cake mix
2 (8 ounce) packages cream cheese, softened
½ cup sugar
2 teaspoons vanilla, divided
2 eggs
⅓ cup sour cream
2 (1 ounce) squares unsweetened chocolate
3 tablespoons butter
1 cup powdered sugar

Preheat oven to 350°. Prepare cake mix according to package directions. Pour batter into 9-inch, springform pan and bake for about 20 minutes. With mixer on medium speed, blend cream cheese, sugar and 1 teaspoon vanilla until smooth and creamy. Add eggs one at a time, beating after each addition. Fold in sour cream and pour on top of cake batter. Bake at 350° for 30 to 35 minutes. Remove from oven and insert knife around edges to loosen. Cool thoroughly and release rim. In small saucepan over low heat, melt chocolate and butter, stirring constantly. Remove from heat and add sugar, 2 tablespoons hot water and remaining 1 teaspoon vanilla and mix well. Pour over top of cake and spread evenly over top. Chill several hours before serving.

KEY LIME PIE

5 egg yolks
1 (14 ounce) can sweetened condensed milk
⅓ cup key lime juice
1 (9-inch) unbaked graham cracker pie crust
1 (8 ounce) container whipped topping

Preheat oven to 350°. Combine eggs, milk and lime juice. Pour in pie crust and bake for 20 minutes. Cool and refrigerate for 2 hours before serving. Top with whipped topping.

COCONUT CREAM PIE

1 (9-inch) baked pie shell

⅔ cup sugar

¼ cup cornstarch

½ teaspoon salt

3 cups milk

4 egg yolks

2 tablespoons butter

2 teaspoons vanilla

¾ cup flaked coconut

Preheat oven to 400°. In medium saucepan combine sugar, cornstarch and salt. Blend milk and egg yolks and add to sugar mixture. Cook over medium heat to boiling, stirring constantly. Boil 1 minute. Remove from heat, add vanilla, butter and coconut. Cool, stirring occasionally. Pour in cooled pie shell. Top with meringue. Be sure to bring meringue to pie crust to seal. Sprinkle with coconut. Bake at 400° for 10 minutes or until light brown.

MERINGUE:

4 egg whites

½ teaspoon vanilla

¼ teaspoon cream of tartar

½ cup sugar

In large bowl, combine egg whites, vanilla and cream of tartar. Beat on high speed until soft peaks form. Slowly add sugar. Mix on high until sugar dissolves.

Banana Cream Pie

1 (8 ounce) package cream cheese, softened
1 (14 ounce) can sweetened condensed milk
⅓ cup fresh lemon juice
4 bananas
1 (9-inch) chocolate pie crust

In large bowl beat cream cheese until light and fluffy. Gradually beat in sweetened condensed milk until mixture is smooth. Slice bananas and dip banana slices in lemon juice. Drain and use half slices to line crust. Reserve other half for topping. Stir remaining lemon juice into cream cheese-filling mixture. Pour filling over bananas. Arrange remaining banana slices on top of filling. Cover and chill for several hours to set.

Chocolate Cream Pie

4 egg yolks
3 cups milk
1½ cups sugar
⅓ cup cornstarch
1 teaspoon salt
2 (1 ounce) squares unsweetened chocolate
1 tablespoon vanilla
1 (9-inch) baked pie shell
3 egg whites, at room temperature
⅓ cup sugar

In saucepan combine sugar, cornstarch and salt. Blend milk and egg yolks and add to sugar mixture. Cook over medium heat and bring to boil, stirring constantly. Boil 1 minute. Remove from heat and add vanilla and melted chocolate. Pour in baked pie shell and prepare meringue. In small bowl with mixer at high speed beat egg whites until foamy. Gradually beat in ⅓ cup sugar and continue beating until stiff peaks form. Spoon on top of chocolate filling and touch crust around edges to seal. Bake at 400° for 10 minutes or until lightly brown.

GERMAN-CHOCOLATE PIE

1 (4 ounce) package German sweet chocolate

¼ cup (1 stick) butter

1 (14½ ounce) can evaporated milk

1½ cups sugar

3 tablespoons cornstarch

⅛ teaspoon salt

2 eggs

1 teaspoon vanilla

1 (10-inch) pie crust, unbaked

1 (3½ ounce) can flaked coconut

½ cup chopped nuts

Melt chocolate with butter over low heat. Gradually blend in milk. In mixing bowl mix sugar, cornstarch and salt thoroughly. Beat in eggs and vanilla. Gradually blend in chocolate mixture. Pour in pie crust. Combine coconut and pecans and sprinkle over filling. Bake for 45 to 50 minutes. Filling will be soft but will set while cooling. Cool at least 4 hours before slicing.

HERSHEY PIE

6 plain Hershey bars

18 large marshmallows

½ cup milk

1 cup whipping cream, whipped

½ cup chopped pecans

½ cup flaked coconut

1 (9-inch) baked pie crust

In double boiler, melt Hershey bars and marshmallows in milk and mix well. Cool and fold in whipped cream and pecans. Pour in pie crust. Refrigerate at least 8 hours before slicing.

CLASSIC CAKES

CHEESECAKE

PASTRY:

1 cup sifted all-purpose flour

2 tablespoons sugar

⅛ teaspoon salt

1 teaspoon grated lemon rind

½ cup (1 stick) butter

1 large egg yolk, slightly beaten

1 teaspoon lemon juice

1 teaspoon ice water

Preheat oven to 400°. In medium bowl blend flour, sugar, salt and lemon rind. With pastry blender, cut in butter, egg, lemon juice and water and mix well. Pat a thin layer of dough in bottom of 10-inch spring form pan. Bake 7 minutes, remove from oven and cool. Attach sides to pan, pat remaining dough evenly around sides or roll the remaining dough out between 2 pieces of wax paper in 3 strips 9 x 2½-inches. Line sides of pan with strips, be careful to seal the strips together and set aside.

CHEESECAKE FILLING:

2½ pounds cream cheese, softened

1¾ cups sugar

2½ tablespoons flour

⅛ teaspoon salt

5 large eggs, plus 2 yolks

½ cup heavy cream

1 teaspoon vanilla extract

2½ teaspoons grated lemon zest

2 egg whites, stiffly beaten

Preheat oven to 475°. In large bowl beat cream cheese until very light and fluffy. Gradually add sugar, flour and salt and mix well after each addition. Add eggs, one at a time, beating well after each addition. Add cream, vanilla and lemon zest and beat until very smooth. Gently fold in egg whites. Carefully pour in crust-lined pan. Bake at 425° for 10 minutes. Reduce temperature to 225° and continue baking 1 hour. Turn off oven and allow cake to sit for 30 minutes in oven with door open ½ inch. Remove from oven and cool completely before chilling. When ready to serve, gently loosen pastry from side of pan and remove sides.

CREAMY CHEESECAKE

PASTRY:

18 graham crackers crushed

2 tablespoons sugar

6 tablespoons butter, melted

Mix graham crackers, sugar and butter and line spring-mold pan.

FILLING:

3 (8 ounce) packages cream cheese, softened

1 cup sugar

4 eggs

2 teaspoons vanilla

Preheat over to 350°. Cream cheese in mixer to fluffy consistency. Slowly add sugar. Add eggs one at a time and beat after each addition. Add vanilla and beat thoroughly. Pour filling in crumb-lined pan. Bake for 35 minutes. Remove from oven and add topping.

TOPPING:

1 pint heavy sour cream

2 teaspoons sugar

1 teaspoon vanilla

Heat oven to 450°. Mix sour cream, sugar and vanilla and spread on top of cheesecake. Bake for 7 minutes.

CHERRY CHEESECAKE

3 tablespoons butter

4 tablespoons sugar

1 cup graham cracker crumbs

4 (8 ounce) packages cream cheese, softened

1 cup sugar

1 cup sour cream

1 tablespoon vanilla

4 tablespoons flour

4 eggs

1 (21 ounce) can cherry pie filling

Preheat oven to 325°. In small saucepan, melt butter and remove from heat. Stir in sugar and graham cracker crumbs until well mixed. Pour into bottom of 9-inch, springform pan. Bake at 325° for about 10 minutes. Remove from oven. Blend cream cheese, sugar and flour with mixer until well mixed and creamy. Stir in eggs, one at a time, and mix thoroughly. Blend in sour cream and vanilla. Pour mixture into graham cracker crust and bake at 425° for 10 minutes. Reduce oven to 250° and continue baking for 1 hour. Remove from oven and cool thoroughly. Insert knife and move around edges of pan to loosen. Release rim and remove from pan. Chill. Pour cherry pie filling over top when ready to serve.

Topping variations: Blueberrry pie filling, fresh strawberries, fresh blueberries or lemon sauce.

CHOCOLATE CAKE

1 cup sugar

⅓ cup shortening

1 egg

2 (1 ounce) squares unsweetened chocolate, melted

1 teaspoon baking soda

1 teaspoon baking powder

1 teaspoon salt

1 cup hot water

1 teaspoon vanilla

1½ cups flour

Preheat oven to 350°. In large bowl, cream sugar and shortening. Add egg and melted chocolate and mix well, using large mixing spoon. Add baking soda, baking powder, salt and flour and mix. Add hot water and mix then add flour and mix. Add vanilla and pour in greased 8-inch square baking dish. Bake at 350° for 30 minutes.

ANGEL FOOD CAKE

1¼ cups sifted cake flour

½ cup sugar, divided

1½ cups (12) egg whites, at room temperature

¼ teaspoon salt

1¼ teaspoons cream of tartar

1 teaspoon vanilla

¼ teaspoon almond extract

1⅓ cups sugar

Sift cake flour with ⅓ cup sugar 4 times. Combine egg whites, salt, cream of tartar, vanilla and almond in large bowl. Beat with a flat wire whip, rotary beater or high speed electric mixer until moist, glossy and soft peaks form. Add 1⅓ cups sugar, sprinkling in ⅓ cup at a time and beating after each addition until well blended (about 25 strokes by hand). Sift flour mixture into egg white mixture in four additions, using 15 strokes to fold over mixture after each addition. Turn bowl often while folding in mixture. After last addition, use 10 to 20 extra strokes. Pour into ungreased 10-inch tube pan. Bake at 375° for 35 to 40 minutes or until the top springs back when pressed lightly. Invert on rack and cool thoroughly. Remove from pan and frost.

BUTTER CREAM FROSTING:

½ cup butter, softened

⅛ teaspoon salt

1 cup powdered sugar

1 egg or 2 egg yolks

1 teaspoon vanilla

2 tablespoons milk

Cream butter and salt, gradually add a little sugar and blend well. Stir in egg and vanilla. Add a little more sugar and beat well. Add a little milk and beat well. Continue adding sugar and milk, beating each after an addition. Beat until frosting reaches a smooth, creamy consistency for spreading. Makes 2½ cups or enough to cover tops and sides of two 9-inch layers, three 8-inch layers, a 9-inch square, a 13 x 9-inch cake or a 10-inch tube cake.

STRAWBERRY SHORTCAKE

1 quart strawberries
Sugar
2 cups biscuit mix
¾ cup milk
3 tablespoons melted butter
2 tablespoons sugar

Wash and stem strawberries. Slice diagonally into medium bowl. Pour enough sugar to cover strawberries. Cover bowl with plastic wrap and chill for several hours. (The longer the strawberries chill, the more juice is in the bowl.)

Preheat oven to 450°. Combine biscuit mix, milk, butter and 2 tablespoons sugar until all biscuit mix is blended with other ingredients. Spread wax paper on counter and lightly dust with flour. Knead dough on wax paper about 8 to 10 times. Roll dough to ½-inch thickness. Cut with floured 3-inch, round cookie cutter or drinking glass with sharp edge. Bake on ungreased baking sheet at 450° for about 10 minutes or until golden brown on top. When ready to serve, slice shortcakes in half, pour strawberries over bottom half and top with whipped topping. Add top half of shortcake and pour more strawberries and whipped topping on top if desired.

½ cup (1 stick) butter

2 cups packed light brown sugar

1 (20 ounce) can pineapple, crushed, drained

10 maraschino cherries, quartered

1 (18.25 ounce) box pineapple cake mix

Preheat oven to 350°. In small saucepan melt butter and brown sugar until creamy.

Divide mixture evenly between 2 (9-inch) cake pans. Spread crushed pineapple and cherries evenly over brown-sugar mixture in each pan. Prepare cake mix according to package directions and pour over brown sugar-pineapple mixture. Bake at 350° for 35 to 40 minutes or until toothpick inserted in center of cake comes out clean. Remove cake from oven and cool for 10 minutes. Put plate on top of cake pan, turn cake pan upside down and tap bottom of cake pan several times with knife. Gently lift cake pan off cake.

Mississippi Mud Cake

1 cup (2 sticks) butter, softened

2 cups sugar

4 eggs

1 teaspoon vanilla

2 tablespoons cocoa

1½ cups flour

1 cup chopped nuts

1 cup flaked coconut

Preheat oven to 350°. Cream butter and sugar. Add eggs and vanilla and beat well. Combine cocoa, flour, nuts and coconut in bowl and mix with spoon. Add to other ingredients and mix well. Pour into greased 9 x 13-inch baking pan. Bake at 350° for 35 to 45 minutes.

Frosting:

1 (7 ounce) jar marshmallow creme

1 (1 pound) box powdered sugar

½ cup (1 stick) butter, softened

½ cup evaporated milk

⅓ cup cocoa

1 teaspoon vanilla

Spoon marshmallow creme over warm cake. Let soften, then spread over cake. Blend softened butter with sugar; add other ingredients and mix well. Spread over marshmallow layer.

Mom's Pound Cake

1 cup (2 sticks) butter, softened

2 cups sugar

5 eggs

2 cups flour

1 tablespoon almond flavoring

Combine all ingredients in mixing bowl and beat for 10 minutes at medium speed.

Pour into greased, floured tube pan. (Batter will be very thick.) Bake at 325° for 1 hour. Test with toothpick for doneness.

Chocolate Pound Cake

1 cup (2 sticks) butter, softened

2 cups sugar

1 cup packed brown sugar

6 large eggs

2½ cups flour

¼ teaspoon baking soda

½ cup cocoa

1 (8 ounce) carton sour cream

2 teaspoons vanilla

Preheat oven to 325°. Grease and flour 10-inch tube pan. Combine in mixing bowl, butter, sugar and brown sugar. Beat with electric mixer about 2 minutes until soft and creamy. Add eggs, beating well. Combine flour, baking soda and cocoa; add to creamed mixture alternately with sour cream and vanilla, beginning and ending with flour mixture. Mix at lowest speed after each addition just until blended. Spoon batter into tube pan and bake for 1 hour and 20 minutes or until toothpick inserted in center of cake comes out clean. Cool in pan for 10 to 15 minutes. Remove from pan and cool on wire rack.

COCONUT CAKE

2½ cups sifted cake flour

1⅔ cups sugar

1 teaspoon salt

3½ teaspoons baking powder

⅔ cup shortening

1¼ cups milk, divided

3 eggs

1 teaspoon vanilla

7-Minute Frosting

½ cup shredded coconut

Combine flour, sugar, salt and baking powder in large bowl. Add shortening and ¾ cup milk. Beat 2 minutes. Add eggs and remaining ½ cup milk and vanilla. Beat 2 minutes longer. Pour equal amounts in 2 greased, papered 9-inch pans. Bake 350° for 35 to 40 minutes. Frost with 7-Minute Frosting and dust with coconut.

7-MINUTE FROSTING:

2 egg whites

5 tablespoons water

1½ cups sugar

1½ teaspoons light corn syrup

1 teaspoon vanilla

Combine egg whites, water, sugar and syrup in top of double boiler. Beat with electric mixer on high speed, continue beating rapidly over boiling water for seven minutes or until frosting will stand in peaks. Remove from heat and add vanilla. Beat again and spread on cake.

♨ CARROT CAKE

4 eggs

2 cups sugar

1⅓ cups oil

2 cups flour

1 teaspoon salt

2 teaspoons baking soda

2 teaspoons baking powder

2 teaspoons ground cinnamon

3 to 4 cups grated carrots

¾ cup chopped pecans

Preheat oven to 325°. Combine sugar and eggs and beat well. Sift flour, salt, baking soda, baking powder and cinnamon together. Add to sugar mixture a little at a time and alternately with oil. Add carrots and nuts. Bake in 3 (8-inch) greased and floured, layer cake pans. Bake for 45 minutes. Remove from oven to cool and frost with Cream Cheese Icing.

CREAM CHEESE FROSTING:

½ cup (1 stick) butter, softened

1 (8 ounce) package cream cheese, softened

1 (16 ounce) box powdered sugar

1 teaspoon vanilla

1 cup chopped nuts

Beat butter and cream cheese. Add powdered sugar and vanilla and beat to mix well. Spread over 3 layers, top and sides of cooled cake.

BANANA NUT BREAD

1 cup sugar

4 tablespoons butter, softened

1 egg

1 cup mashed bananas

1½ cups flour

½ teaspoon baking soda

½ cup chopped nuts

Preheat oven to 350°. Cream sugar and butter, add egg and beat until smooth. Add all other ingredients and mix well. Bake in greased, floured loaf pan for 50 to 60 minutes.

CRUMB CAKE

2 cups packed brown sugar

2½ cups flour, sifted

Pinch salt

½ cup shortening

Mix sugar, flour, salt and shortening until it is crumbly. Remove ¾ cup crumbs for topping.

2 eggs

1 cup buttermilk

1 teaspoon baking soda

1 teaspoon vanilla

Preheat oven to 350°. Add remaining crumbs to eggs, buttermilk, baking soda (dissolved in a little milk) and vanilla. Beat well, place in greased, floured loaf pan. Spread crumbs on top. Bake 45 to 55 minutes or until tester inserted in center comes out clean.

Fresh Apple Cake

2 cups unsifted all-purpose flour

2 cups sugar

2 teaspoons baking soda

1 teaspoon cinnamon

½ teaspoon nutmeg

½ teaspoon salt

4 cups tart apples, pared, finely diced

½ cup chopped walnuts

½ cup (1 stick) butter, softened

2 eggs

Powdered sugar

Preheat oven to 325°. In large bowl, sift flour, sugar, baking soda, cinnamon, nutmeg and salt. Add apples, nuts, butter and eggs. Beat until well blended. Pour in 9 x 13-inch baking dish and bake 50 minutes or until top springs back when lightly touched. Cool slightly in pan on wire rack. Sprinkle with powdered sugar and serve warm. Cut in squares and top with whipped cream or ice cream.

Golden Butter Cake

1 cup (2 sticks) butter

2 cups sugar

3 eggs

2 cups flour

2 tablespoons orange juice

Preheat oven to 350°. Cream sugar and butter until light and fluffy. Add eggs one at a time and beat after each addition. Stir in flour and orange juice. Pour into greased, floured bundt cake or tube cake pan. Bake at 350° for about 1 hour. Cake is done when toothpick or cake tester is inserted in center and comes out clean.

1 (18 ounce) box yellow cake mix with
   pudding
3 eggs
⅓ cup oil
½ cup rum
1 cup chopped pecans

Mix cake mix, eggs, water, oil and rum in mixing bowl and blend well. Stir in pecans. Pour into greased and floured 10-inch tube or bundt pan. Bake at 325° for 1 hour. (If you want a sweeter cake, sprinkle powdered sugar over top of cooled cake.)

POPPY SEED CAKE

3 cups sugar

1¼ cups shortening

6 eggs

3 cups flour

¼ teaspoon baking soda

½ teaspoon salt

1 cup buttermilk

3 tablespoons poppy seeds

2 teaspoons almond extract

2 teaspoons vanilla

2 teaspoons butter flavoring

In large mixing bowl, cream sugar and shortening until mixture is light and fluffy. Add eggs, one at a time, blending mixture well. Sift flour, baking soda and salt. Alternately add dry ingredients and buttermilk to the sugar mixture. Add poppy seeds and flavoring and blend well. Pour in greased, floured bundt pan. Cook for 1 hour and 15 to 20 minutes. Test with toothpick for doneness. Top with glaze.

GLAZE:

1½ cups powdered sugar

⅓ cup lemon juice

1 teaspoon vanilla

1 teaspoon almond extract

Combine powdered sugar lemon juice, vanilla and almond extract and mix well. Pour over top cooled cake.

4 ounces Baker's chocolate

6 eggs, separated

¾ cup sugar

⅓ teaspoon salt

1 cup powdered sugar, sifted

1½ cups butter

1 teaspoon vanilla

30 lady fingers, split

1 cup heavy cream, whipped

1 teaspoon instant coffee

1 teaspoon powdered sugar

Melt chocolate in double boiler. Beat egg yolks until lemon-colored. Gradually beat in sugar until smooth and thick. Beat in milk. Add egg mixture to chocolate. Cook, stirring until well blended, 5 to 10 minutes. Let cool in large mixing bowl for 30 minutes. Add salt to egg whites, beat until stiff but not dry. Beat ½ cup powdered sugar, 1 tablespoon at a time. Reserve. Cream butter, gradually beat in rest of powdered sugar. Add to chocolate mixture and stir until well blended. Gently fold in egg whites and vanilla. Line bottom and sides of 3-quart springform with a single layer of lady fingers and place them vertically around sides. Pour in ⅓ of chocolate mixture, then another layer of lady fingers. There will be 3 layers. Refrigerate overnight. Next day wrap and freeze. Just before serving, add whipped cream, flavored with coffee and sugar, to the top. If frozen allow 8 hours to thaw in refrigerator. Two hours before serving, remove spring form.

CHOCOLATE CUPCAKES

3 cups flour

2 cups sugar

½ cup cocoa

2 teaspoons baking soda

1 teaspoon salt

2 cups water

⅔ cup oil

2 tablespoons vinegar

1 teaspoon vanilla

Mix all ingredients well. Put cupcake papers in muffin tins and fill papers half full of batter.

1 (8 ounce) cream cheese, softened

1 egg

½ cup sugar

⅛ teaspoon salt

1 cup chocolate chips

Preheat oven to 350°. Mix cream cheese, egg, sugar and salt and beat well. Stir in chocolate chips. Put generous tablespoon of topping on top of each cupcake. Bake for 25 minutes. Makes 3 dozen.

CHOCOLATE PUDDING CAKE

1 milk chocolate cake mix
1¼ cups milk
⅓ cup oil
3 eggs

Combine all ingredients in a mixing bowl. Beat well. Pour into a greased and buttered 9 x 13-inch baking pan. Bake at 350° for 35 minutes or until cake tester comes out clean.

FROSTING:

1 can sweetened condensed milk
¾ (16 ounce) can chocolate syrup
1 (8 ounce) carton whipped topping, thawed
⅓ cup chopped pecans

In a small bowl mix the sweetened condensed milk and chocolate syrup. Pour over cake and let soak into cake. Chill for several hours. Spread whipped topping over top of cake and sprinkle pecans over the top. Refrigerate.

CREAM PUFFS

½ cup butter
1 cup boiling water
1 cup sifted flour
¼ teaspoon salt
4 eggs

Preheat oven to 450°. Melt butter in boiling water. Add flour and salt all at once. Stir vigorously with wooden spoon over medium-high heat. Watch for scorching. Cook and stir until mixture forms a ball that doesn't separate. Remove from heat. Allow to cool slightly. Using metal spoon, add eggs one at a time, beating well after each addition. On greased cookie sheet spoon 2½-inch mounds 2-inches apart. Bake at 450° for 12 minutes then reduce heat to 325° for 20–25 minutes.

FILLING:

½ pint heavy cream, whipped
2 teaspoons sugar
1 teaspoon vanilla

Whip cream. Add sugar and vanilla. Beat stiff. Fill puffs.

CUSTARD FILLING:

3 tablespoons cornstarch
½ cup sugar
⅛ teaspoon salt
½ cup cold milk
1½ cups milk, scalded
1 teaspoon vanilla
2 egg yolks with 2 tablespoons milk

Mix cornstarch, sugar, salt and cold milk. Gradually add hot milk. Boil, stirring until thick. Don't BURN. Stir some of hot mixture over the yolks, then add yolks to custard. Stir well. Add vanilla. If desired a tablespoon of butter may be added at this point. Cool slightly and fill cream puffs.

2 squares unsweetened chocolate

1 to 2½ cups powdered sugar

1 teaspoon vanilla

2 tablespoons butter

Melt butter and chocolate together. Add sugar and vanilla stirring until smooth. If needed, milk may be added to improve spreading consistency. Drizzle over tops of filled cream puffs.

Cream puffs may be frozen in an airtight container filled with ice cream or whipped cream for 2 months.

CHOCOLATE-FILLED CREAM PUFFS

1 cup water

½ cup (1 stick) butter

1 cup flour

4 eggs

1 (22 ounce) plus 1 (8 ounce) container
   chocolate pudding (3 to 4 cups)

1 cup milk chocolate chips, melted

Preheat oven to 400°. Combine water and butter in medium saucepan and bring to a boil. When butter melts, remove pan from heat. Stir in flour until mixture forms a ball and pulls away from sides of pan. Beat in eggs until mixture is smooth. (At first it will appear sort of curdled, but after you begin to beat it, it will become very smooth). Drop by rounded tablespoonfuls onto ungreased baking sheet. Bake for 35 minutes or until cream puffs are well browned. Remove from oven and cool to room temperature. Cut tops off cream puffs and set aside. Fill with chocolate pudding and replace tops. Drizzle melted chocolate over each cream puff.

Tip: Cream puff shells keep very well. Make them the day before and fill them the day you need them, so they will be very fresh and not soggy. If you are not going to fill the shells immediately, keep them covered or in a sealed plastic bag once they have completely cooled.

Tip: As an alternative to using a pastry bag it is easy to fill cream puffs by putting the pudding in a sturdy plastic bag and cutting about ½ inch off the corner. This makes a handy, neat way to pipe the pudding into the puffs. Do this with chocolate as well. Put chips in bag and melt them in the microwave on HALF power for about 2 minutes, kneading bag after each minute. Snip off a tiny corner of bag and squeeze melted chocolate out in a steady stream over the cream puffs.

Custard Filling:

Additional fillings may be used with these cream puffs and here is one that is delicious.

3 egg yolks
½ cup sugar
2 tablespoons cornstarch
2 cups half-and-half

Combine egg yolks, sugar and cornstarch in top of double boiler over simmering water.

Stir to blend into smooth paste and gradually add half-and-half as you stir.

Cook, stirring frequently, for 10 to 12 minutes until mixture thickens to the consistency of pudding. Remove from heat and cool before filling cream puffs.

Puddings, Cobblers & Ice Creams

🎋 RICE PUDDING

2 cups cooked rice

1½ cups milk

2½ cups evaporated milk

4½ cups sugar

2 large eggs, beaten

½ teaspoon baking soda

2 teaspoons vanilla

4 (4-inch) sticks cinnamon

¼ cup seedless golden raisins

Cook rice according to package directions. Rinse rice thoroughly with cold water immediately after removing from heat. In top of large double boiler, mix milk, evaporated milk, sugar, eggs, baking soda and vanilla and bring to rapid boil over direct heat stirring constantly. Remove from heat, stir in cooked rice and cut cinnamon sticks in center. Return to heat and cook over water boiling at medium heat for 1 hour. Remove from heat and add raisins. Do not add raisins during cooking time because milk will curdle. Pour pudding in serving bowl and chill before serving.

🎋 CREAMY BANANA PUDDING

1 (14 ounce) can sweetened condensed milk

1½ cups cold water

1 (3¼ ounce) package instant vanilla
   pudding mix

1 (8 ounce) carton whipped topping

36 vanilla wafers

3 ripe bananas

In large bowl, combine sweetened condensed milk and water. Add pudding mix and beat well. Chill for 5 minutes. Fold in whipped topping and spoon 1 cup pudding mixture into 3-quart glass serving bowl. Top with one-third of each: wafers, bananas and pudding. Repeat layering twice, ending with pudding. Cover and chill.

BREAD PUDDING

1 (1-pound) loaf raisin-cinnamon bread

4 tablespoons butter, softened

4 eggs, beaten

1 cup sugar

1 teaspoon vanilla

¼ teaspoon salt

3 cups milk, scalded

Preheat oven to 350°. Cut sliced bread into cubes. Place in buttered, 3-quart baking dish. Beat eggs, sugar, vanilla and salt until blended. Stir in hot milk and pour over bread. Allow mixture to set until bread cubes absorb liquid. Gently mix and bake for 50 to 55 minutes or until set.

Variations: Add fresh blueberries, cranberries or additional raisins to give a little more flavor. Sauces are also wonderful including the Whiskey Sauce below.

WHISKEY SAUCE:

½ cup butter

1 cup sugar

1 egg, well beaten

Whiskey to taste

In top of double boiler, heat sugar and butter until very hot and completely dissolved. Add egg and beat quickly so egg does not curdle. Cool and add whiskey to taste.

CREAMY CHOCOLATE MOUSSE

What a dreamy delight! This thick, velvety smooth mousse is a favorite every time.

1 (12 ounce) package semi-sweet chocolate
  chips
3 cups heavy whipping cream, divided
2 tablespoons orange liqueur
⅓ cup powdered sugar

Combine chocolate chips and 1 cup whipping cream in heavy, medium saucepan. Cook over low to medium heat, stirring constantly, until chocolate melts and mixture is smooth. Stir in orange liqueur. Set aside and cool to room temperature. In large bowl, beat remaining 2 cups whipping cream and powdered sugar until stiff peaks form. Gently fold in chocolate mixture until well blended and evenly colored. Spoon into 8 dessert cups. Cover and chill for several hours or until ready to serve.

Optional: For a really nice finish, garnish each dessert with a pretty cookie such as a pirouette to give it a little extra flair. Top with dollop of whipped cream and place a chocolate-dipped, candied, orange peel or chocolate-covered strawberry on top.

BLUEBERRY COBBLER

½ cup (1 stick) butter, melted
1 cup self-rising flour
1¾ cups sugar
1 cup milk
1 (21 ounce) can blueberry pie filling

Pour butter in 9-inch baking pan. Mix flour and sugar in bowl and slowly pour milk in and stir. Pour flour, sugar and milk over butter and spoon pie filling over batter. Bake at 300° for 1 hour. Top with whipped cream to serve.

❧ PEACH COBBLER

3 cups sliced fresh peaches

1 tablespoon lemon juice

¼ teaspoon almond extract

1 cup sifted flour

1 cup sugar

½ teaspoon salt

1 egg, beaten

6 tablespoons butter, melted

Preheat oven to 375°. Butter 10 x 6-inch baking dish and place peaches on bottom. Sprinkle with lemon juice and almond extract. In separate bowl, sift flour and add sugar and salt. With fork stir in eggs and mix until crumbly. Sprinkle over peaches and drizzle with melted butter. Bake 35 to 40 minutes.

❧ APPLE CRISP

5 cups peeled, cored, sliced apples

½ cup (1 stick) butter, melted

1 cup quick-cooking oats

½ cup firmly packed brown sugar

⅓ cup flour

Preheat over to 375°. Place apple slices in 8 x 8-inch or 9 x 9-inch square baking pan. Combine all ingredients and sprinkle mixture over apples. Bake at 375° for 40 to 45 minutes or until apples are tender and topping is brown.

Optional: Add 1 teaspoon cinnamon and ½ cup raisins or dried cranberries to apples before sprinkling with topping.

❧ SPECIAL PEACH CRISP

4¾ cups peeled, sliced peaches

3 tablespoons lemon juice

1 cup flour

1¾ cups sugar

1 egg, beaten

Place peaches in 9-inch baking dish and sprinkle lemon juice over top. Mix flour, sugar, egg and dash of salt. Spread mixture over top of peaches. Dot with a little butter. Bake at 375° until golden brown.

❧ PEACH CRUMB

1 (21 ounce) can peach pie filling

½ cup quick-cooking oats

½ cup flour

½ cup firmly packed brown sugar

½ cup (1 stick) butter, melted

Preheat oven at 350°. Pour peach pie filling in 8 x 8-inch baking dish. In medium bowl, combine oats, flour and brown sugar. Stir in butter until mixture is thoroughly blended.

Sprinkle mixture evenly over peach pie filling. Bake for 40 to 45 minutes or until topping is brown.

❧ CHERRY CRUNCH

1 (1 pound 5 ounce) can cherry pie filling

1 teaspoon lemon juice

1 (18.5 ounce) white cake mix

½ cup chopped nuts

½ cup (1 stick) butter

Preheat oven to 350°. Spread pie filling over bottom of 9 x 13-inch baking dish. Sprinkle with lemon juice. Combine cake mix, nuts and butter and sprinkle over pie filling. Bake for 45 to 50 minutes or until golden brown. Serve with ice cream or whipped cream.

MAPLE CRÈME BRÛLÉE

4 egg yolks
½ cup maple syrup
2½ cups half-and-half
2½ teaspoons sugar, divided

Preheat oven to 350°. In medium bowl, whisk egg yolks with maple syrup, half-and-half and 1½ teaspoons sugar. Divide egg yolk mixture among custard cups. Place 6 crème brulee dishes or custard cups in large baking dish. Pour enough hot water into large baking dish to come halfway up sides of cups. Bake at 350° for 40 to 45 minutes or until custard is set and knife inserted in middle comes out clean. Remove from water bath, cool on rack and chill. When ready to serve, sprinkle about 1 teaspoon sugar evenly over surface of each and place under broiler. Broil until sugar melts slightly and forms a crisp coating.

Cool again or chill for a few minutes and serve.

BAKED CUSTARD

5 tablespoons sugar
3 eggs
⅛ teaspoon salt
½ teaspoon vanilla
2 cups milk, scalded

Mix sugar, eggs, salt and vanilla and combine with milk. Pour in custard cups or baking dish. Set in baking pan of hot water and bake until firm, about 30 to 40 minutes or until a knife inserted in center comes out clean.

ALMOND CUSTARD WITH CHOCOLATE SAUCE

Simply delicious!

3 cups heavy whipping cream, divided
½ cup sugar
6 egg yolks
¼ teaspoon almond extract
3 (1 ounce) squares semi-sweet baking
 chocolate

Combine 2½ cups cream and sugar in medium saucepan, bring to boil over medium heat and stir frequently. Immediately remove from heat and cool to room temperature. Preheat oven to 350° and place 6 custard cups in 9 x 13-inch baking dish. Whisk egg yolks and almond extract into cream mixture, just until blended. (Try not to make it frothy.) Ladle cream mixture into custard cups and fill each evenly. Place baking dish in oven and make water bath by adding enough hot water to baking dish to bring water level halfway up sides of custard cups. Bake for 40 to 45 minutes until centers are set, but loose and knife inserted in center comes out clean. Remove from oven and place custard cups on cooling rack to cool. Cover and chill until ready to serve. To serve, turn custard out of custard dish onto plate. Loosen custard first by running sharp knife around edges. Drizzle chocolate sauce over top of each custard before serving.

CHOCOLATE SAUCE:

Combine remaining ½ cup whipping cream and chocolate in small saucepan. Cook over low heat, stirring constantly, until chocolate melts and mixture is smooth and slightly thick. Remove from heat and cool to room temperature. Put in covered container and chill until ready to use. Makes about ¾ cup.

Variation: Sprinkle toasted, slivered almonds on top.

❧ Hot Fudge Sundae

1 cup semi-sweet chocolate chips

1 tablespoon butter

¼ cup sugar

½ cup evaporated milk

vanilla ice cream

chopped nuts

whipped topping

maraschino cherries

In heavy saucepan over low heat, melt chocolate, butter and sugar, stirring constantly. Remove from heat, pour in milk and stir until smooth. In separate bowl, place 1 or 2 scoops vanilla ice cream, pour hot fudge over top, sprinkle nuts, whipped topping and maraschino cherry on top. Serve immediately.

Variations: Variations are numerous and here are just a few ideas. Put a brownie in the bowl with ice cream, hot fudge sauce, nuts, whipped topping and cherry on top. Slice fresh strawberries, cover with sugar and chill for 3 or 4 hours. Pour strawberries and juice on top. Try any of the following: coconut, heated peanut butter, butterscotch sauce, caramel sauce, pineapple sauce, 10 or 12 halved maraschino cherries and cherry juice, chopped candy bars and cookie crumbs.

❧ Creamy Peach Parfait Topped with Almonds

1 (3 ounce) package cream cheese, softened

1 (14 ounce) can sweetened condensed milk

⅓ cup lemon juice

1 (20 ounce) can peach pie filling

¼ cup sliced almonds, toasted

In medium bowl, beat cream cheese until light and fluffy. Gradually stir in sweetened condensed milk and lemon juice and blend well. Into each parfait glass, spoon about 1 tablespoon cheese mixture and about 2 tablespoons pie filling. Repeat layering. Top with dollop of cheese mixture and sliced, toasted almonds.

♨ RED, WHITE AND GOOEY BANANA SPLITS

Sometimes we forget the simplest things, so we added a banana split to this collection. The fun part is in the variations we suggest and you invent.

1 firm banana
1 scoop each: vanilla, chocolate,
    strawberry ice cream
2 tablespoons each: chocolate syrup,
    strawberry syrup, butterscotch sauce
Whipped cream
Maraschino cherries

Peel banana and slice in 2 pieces lengthwise. Put 1 scoop each of vanilla, chocolate and strawberry ice cream between slices of banana. Pour chocolate syrup, strawberry syrup and butterscotch sauce over scoops of ice cream. Top with whipped cream and maraschino cherry. Optional: Finely chopped nuts sprinkled over the top are really great!

Variation: Try neapolitan ice cream instead of chocolate, vanilla and strawberry.

Variation: Invent your own special ice cream and topping selections. Top with sprinkles, Red Hots, chocolate chips, peanut butter chips, brickle chips, M & M's, candy bars, cookies, almond slivers and the list goes on. What will you come up with to make this a memorable dessert?

❧ Easy Chocolate Sauce

½ cup whipping cream
3 (1 ounce) squares semi-sweet baking
   chocolate

Combine whipping cream and chocolate in small saucepan. Cook over low heat, stirring constantly, until chocolate melts and mixture is smooth and slightly thick. Remove from heat and cool to room temperature. If not used immediately, place in covered container and chill until ready to use. Warm slightly in microwave, if necessary, before using. Yields about ¾ cup.

❧ Hot Fudge Sauce

2 cups chocolate chips
½ cup half-and-half
½ teaspoon vanilla

Combine chocolate chips and half-and-half in small saucepan over very low heat. Stir constantly until chocolate melts and mixture is smooth. Remove from heat and stir in vanilla. Serve warm. Keep remaining sauce chilled. When ready to use again, warm slightly in microwave and stir after every 30 seconds, until it can be poured.

COOKIES, BROWNIES & FUDGE

Gingerbread

5¼ cups flour

⅓ cup sugar

1 cup dark molasses

¾ cup hot water

½ cup shortening

1 egg

1 teaspoon baking soda

1 teaspoon ginger

1 teaspoon cinnamon

½ teaspoon salt

Preheat oven to 325°. In large bowl combine flour, sugar, molasses, hot water, shortening, egg, baking soda, ginger, cinnamon and salt and mix well. Pour in greased, floured 9 x 9-inch baking dish. Bake 40 to 50 minutes at 325°. Serve warm and top with whipped cream or butter.

Easy Sugar Cookies

1 (8 ounce) package cream cheese, softened

¾ cup sugar

1 cup (2 sticks) butter

½ teaspoon lemon extract

2½ cups flour

In medium bowl, combine cream cheese with sugar, butter and lemon extract. Beat until well blended. Add flour and mix thoroughly. Cover and chill several hours or overnight. When ready to bake, preheat oven to 375° and roll dough out on lightly floured surface to ⅛-inch thickness. Cut shapes with cookie cutter and place on ungreased baking sheet. Bake 6 to 8 minutes. Remove from oven and let cookies cool for 1 minute on baking sheet then transfer to cooling rack.

Optional: Before baking, lightly brush cookies with beaten egg and sprinkle with colored sugar or candy.

BROWN-SUGAR COOKIES

1 cup (2 sticks) butter, softened
¾ cup packed dark brown sugar
1 egg yolk
1 tablespoon vanilla
1¼ cups flour

Preheat oven to 325°. In mixing bowl, beat butter and gradually add brown sugar. Add egg yolk and vanilla and beat well. Add flour and dash salt slowly and mix well. Shape dough in 1-inch balls and chill 2 hours. Place cookie dough on baking sheet and flatten each cookie with back of spoon. Bake at 350° for 10 to 12 minutes.

TOLL HOUSE CHOCOLATE CHIP COOKIES

2¼ cups unsifted all-purpose flour
1 teaspoon baking soda
1 teaspoon salt
1 cup (2 sticks) butter, softened
¾ cup sugar
¾ cup firmly packed brown sugar
1 teaspoon vanilla
2 eggs
1 (12 ounce) package semi-sweet,
     real chocolate morsels
1 cup chopped nuts

In large bowl combine butter, sugar, brown sugar and vanilla and stir until creamy. Add eggs and mix thoroughly. Add flour mixture a little at a time and stir to mix well. Add chocolate morsels and nuts and mix. Drop by rounded teaspoonfuls onto ungreased baking sheets. Bake at 350° for 8 to 10 minutes. (The longer the cookies bake, the crispier they will be.)

❧ OATMEAL COOKIES

1 cup packed brown sugar

1 cup sugar

1 cup shortening

2 eggs

2 tablespoons water

2 teaspoons vanilla

½ teaspoon salt

1 teaspoon baking soda

1½ cups flour

3 cups quick-cooking oats

1 cup chopped pecans

Preheat oven to 350°. In mixing bowl, combine brown sugar, sugar, shortening, eggs, water and vanilla and beat well. Add salt and baking soda and mix. Add oats and pecans and mix well. Drop by teaspoonfuls on cookie sheet and bake for 14 to 15 minutes.

Variation: Add 1 cup flaked coconut.

ꙮ Oatmeal-Raisin Cookies

1¼ cups all-purpose flour

1 teaspoon baking soda

¾ teaspoon ground cinnamon

½ cup salt

1 cup (2 sticks) butter, softened

¾ cup sugar

¾ cup packed brown sugar

1 teaspoon vanilla extract

2 large eggs

3 cups quick-cooking oats

1 (14 ounce) package raisins

1 cup chopped nuts

Preheat oven to 375°. In small bowl, combine flour, baking soda, cinnamon and salt. Beat butter, sugar, brown sugar and vanilla in large mixing bowl until creamy. Beat in eggs and gradually beat in flour mixture. Stir in oats, raisins and nuts. Drop by rounded tablespoon on ungreased cookie sheet. For chewy cookies bake at 375° for 7 to 8 minutes. For crispy cookies bake 9 to 10 minutes. Cool before serving.

✎ SHORTBREAD COOKIES

2 cups (4 sticks) butter, softened
1 cup powdered sugar
4 cups flour
Additional powdered sugar

Preheat oven to 350°. Cream butter until light and fluffy. Gradually add sugar and beat vigorously after each addition until sugar completely dissolves. Add flour, a little at a time, beating well after each addition. Chill dough for 1 hour. Sprinkle surface with equal parts of flour and powdered sugar and turn one-third of dough at a time onto surface. Pat into thickness of ½ inch and cut cookies with 1½-inch biscuit cutter. Place on ungreased cookie sheet and prick tops of cookies with fork to make a design. Bake 15 to 20 minutes or until lightly golden. Remove from oven and cool slightly before dusting lightly with powdered sugar.

✎ PEANUT BUTTER COOKIES

1 cup (2 sticks) butter, softened
¾ cup peanut butter
1 cup packed light brown sugar
2 large eggs
2 teaspoons vanilla
2½ cups all-purpose flour
2 teaspoons baking soda
½ teaspoon salt
½ cup sugar

Preheat oven to 350°. In large mixing bowl, mix butter, peanut butter, sugar and brown sugar until creamy. Beat in eggs and vanilla. Combine, flour, baking soda, salt and sugar. Drop by rounded tablespoonfuls onto ungreased cookie sheet. Press cookies down twice with fork and make a criss-cross pattern. Bake 9 to 11 minutes. Cool on cookie sheet for several minutes and remove to wire rack to cool completely.

LEMON BARS

¾ cup (1¼ sticks) butter, softened

½ cups sugar

½ cup packed brown sugar

1½ cups flour

1 teaspoon baking powder

½ teaspoon salt

1 cup quick-cooking oatmeal

1 (14 ounce) can sweetened condensed milk

½ cup lemon juice

Preheat oven to 350°. In mixing bowl cream butter, sugar and brown sugar. Add flour, baking powder, salt and oatmeal and beat until mixture is crumbly. Spread half mixture in 9 x 13-inch baking pan, pat down and set remaining mixture aside. In separate bowl mix sweetened condensed milk and lemon juice and stir until thoroughly mixed. Pour over crumbs in baking pan and cover with remaining crumbs. Bake at 350° for 25 minutes. Cool at room temperature, cut in squares and chill.

EVERYDAY SPECIAL BROWNIES

1 cup butter

1½ cups dark chocolate pieces

3 eggs

1¼ cups sugar

1 cup flour

Preheat oven to 350°. Melt butter and chocolate in double boiler over low heat. Cool to room temperature. Beat eggs to foamy in medium bowl. Stir in sugar and beat at medium speed for 2 to 3 minutes. Reduce speed and slowly pour in chocolate-butter mixture. Slowly pour in flour a little at a time. Pour into greased, floured 9 x 13-inch baking pan. Bake for 35 to 45 minutes or until brownies are done in middle. Cool and cut into squares.

♆ THE ULTIMATE BROWNIE

⅔ cup butter

5 (1 ounce) squares unsweetened baking
   chocolate, chopped

1¾ cups sugar

2 teaspoons vanilla

3 eggs

1 cup flour

1 cup chopped nuts

Chocolate Frosting

Preheat oven to 350º. Melt butter and chocolate in saucepan over low heat, stirring constantly. Beat sugar, vanilla and eggs in medium bowl at high speed 5 minutes. Beat in chocolate mixture at low speed. Beat in flour until blended. Stir in nuts. Spread in 9 x 9-inch sprayed baking pan. Bake 35 to 40 minutes or until brownies pull away from sides of pan. Cool and spread with Chocolate Frosting. Cut into squares.

CHOCOLATE FROSTING:

4 tablespoons butter

2 ounces unsweetened baking chocolate

2 cups powdered sugar

4 tablespoons hot water

Melt butter and chocolate in saucepan over low heat, stirring constantly. Remove from heat and stir in powdered sugar and hot water to spreading consistency.

UNBELIEVABLE BROWNIES

1 cup (2 sticks) butter

4 (1 ounce) squares unsweetened chocolate

2½ cups sugar, divided

4 eggs, divided

1 cup flour

2 teaspoons vanilla, divided

1 cup ricotta cheese

1 cup chopped walnuts

Preheat oven to 350°. Melt butter and chocolate in large saucepan. With wire whisk, beat in 2 cups sugar and 3 eggs until blended. Set aside remaining sugar and egg. Stir in flour and 1 teaspoon vanilla. In separate bowl, combine ricotta, remaining sugar, egg and vanilla and beat well. Gently blend cheese mixture into chocolate mixture. Spread batter into sprayed 9 x 13-inch pan. Sprinkle with chopped nuts. Bake for about 45 minutes. Cool, cut in squares and serve.

CHEERLEADER BROWNIES

Great, great brownies!

⅔ cup oil

⅓ cup corn syrup

½ cup cocoa

½ teaspoon salt

1 cup chopped nuts

2 cups sugar

4 eggs, beaten

1½ cups flour

1 teaspoon baking powder

2 teaspoons vanilla

Preheat oven to 350°. In large bowl combine oil, sugar, corn syrup and eggs and mix well. In separate bowl, mix cocoa, flour, salt and baking powder. Pour flour mixture into sugar-egg mixture, a little at a time, mixing after each addition. Add vanilla and nuts and beat well. Pour into greased, floured 7 x 11-inch baking pan and bake at 350° for 45 minutes or until toothpick inserted in center comes out clean. (Do not overcook.) Serve immediately.

⟡ Super Brownies

⅔ cup oil

2 cups sugar

⅓ cup corn syrup

3 eggs, slightly beaten

2 teaspoons vanilla

½ cup cocoa

1½ cups flour

½ teaspoon salt

1 teaspoon baking powder

1 cup chopped pecans

Preheat oven to 350°. In mixing bowl, beat oil, sugar, corn syrup, eggs, and vanilla. Add cocoa, flour, salt and baking powder and beat well. Stir in chopped pecans. Pour in greased, floured 9 x 13-inch baking dish. Bake at 350° for 35 minutes. Brownies are done when toothpick inserted in center comes out clean.

Icing:

¼ cup (½ stick) butter, melted

2 cups powdered sugar

⅓ cup cocoa

1 tablespoon milk

1 teaspoon vanilla

In small saucepan over low heat melt butter, add powdered sugar, cocoa, milk and vanilla and beat until smooth. Spread over brownies.

CRUNCHY PEANUT BUTTER BROWNIES

1 cup (2 sticks) butter

2 cups sugar

6 tablespoons unsweetened cocoa

2 teaspoons vanilla

4 eggs

1 cup flour

½ teaspoon salt

Topping (below)

Preheat oven to 350º. In mixing bowl, cream butter, sugar, cocoa and vanilla until smooth. Add eggs, one at a time, and beat well after each addition. Fold in flour and salt. Spread mixture in sprayed 9 x 13-inch baking pan. Bake at 350º for 25 minutes. Remove from oven and cool.

TOPPING FOR CRUNCHY PEANUT BUTTER BROWNIES

1 (7 ounce) jar marshmallow cream

1 cup chunky or smooth peanut butter

1 (12 ounce) package chocolate chips

3 cups crispy rice cereal

After brownies cool, spread marshmallow cream evenly over top of brownies. In large heavy saucepan over low to medium heat, melt peanut butter and chocolate chips together, stirring constantly. Remove from heat and fold in crispy rice cereal. Spoon peanut butter-chocolate mixture over marshmallow cream and spread evenly. Chill several hours, cut into squares and serve.

SNICKER BROWNIES

1 (18 ounce) box German chocolate cake mix
¾ cup (1½ sticks) butter, melted
½ cup evaporated milk
4 (2.7 ounce) Snicker candy bars

Preheat oven to 350°. In large bowl combine cake mix, butter and evaporated milk. Beat on low speed until well blended. Pour half the batter into greased, floured 9 x 13-inch baking pan. Bake at 350° for 10 minutes. Cut Snicker bars in ⅛-inch slices. Remove from oven and place candy bar slices evenly over brownies. Drop remaining half of batter by spoonfuls over candy bars and spread as evenly as possible. Return to oven and bake for 20 minutes longer. Cool and cut into squares.

GERMAN CHOCOLATE BROWNIE BARS

1 (14 ounce) package caramels, unwrapped
1 (12 ounce) can evaporated milk, divided
1 (18.25 ounce) box German chocolate
   cake mix
1 cup chopped pecans
1 cup semi-sweet chocolate chips

Preheat oven to 350°. Combine caramels with ⅓ cup evaporated milk in top of double boiler set over simmering water. Stir until caramels melt and mixture is smooth. Remove from heat and set aside. In large bowl, combine cake mix with pecans and remaining evaporated milk.

Spread half of batter in bottom of greased 9 x 13-inch baking pan. Bake for 6 minutes. Remove from oven and sprinkle with chocolate chips, then drizzle caramel mixture evenly over top. Drop remaining half of batter by spoonfuls over caramel mixture. Bake 15 to 20 minutes more. Remove from oven and cool before cutting.

FAVORITE FUDGE

4½ cups sugar
1 (12 ounce) can evaporated milk
1 cup (2 sticks) butter
3 (6 ounce) packages chocolate chips
1 tablespoon vanilla
1½ cups chopped pecans

Bring sugar and milk to rolling boil that cannot be stirred down. Boil exactly 6 minutes, stirring constantly. Remove from heat, add butter and chocolate chips, stir until butter and chips melt. Add vanilla and pecans and stir well. Pour in buttered 9 x 13-inch dish. Allow to stand at least 6 hours or overnight before cutting. Store in airtight container.

NEVER-FAIL FUDGE

2 cups sugar
3 tablespoons cocoa
⅔ cup milk
1 package walnuts or pecans, chopped
2 tablespoons butter
1 teaspoon vanilla

In large heavy saucepan blend sugar and cocoa. Add milk and stir until smooth. Cook over medium heat and do not stir after candy begins to boil. Cook candy until a soft ball forms when dropped in cold water. Remove from heat and add nuts, butter and vanilla. Cool until bottom of pan is cool to the touch. Beat until candy is not glossy. Pour in greased 8 x 4-inch baking dish.

 DIVINITY

2½ cups sugar

½ cup light corn syrup

½ cup water

¼ teaspoon salt

2 egg whites

1 teaspoon vanilla

1 cup chopped pecans

In 2-quart saucepan, combine sugar, corn syrup, water and salt. Cook over medium heat, stirring constantly until mixture comes to boil. Reduce heat and cook, without stirring until temperature reaches 265° or until small amount of syrup dropped in cold water holds its shape, yet pliable. Just before temperature reaches 265°, in large bowl beat egg whites until stiff peaks form when beater is raised. Beating constantly on high speed of electric mixer, very slowly pour hot syrup over egg whites. Continue beating until small amounts hold soft peak when dropped from spoon. Mix in vanilla and pecans. Work quickly and drop by teaspoonfuls on wax paper.

Tip: It is better to wait for a sunny day to make divinity.

 PEANUT BUTTER KRISPY TREATS

¼ cup (½ stick) butter

1 (10 ounce) package marshmallows

½ cup peanut crunchy

6 cups Rice Krispies cereal

Melt butter in large saucepan over low heat. Add marshmallows and peanut butter and stir until completely melted. Remove from heat. Add Rice Krispies and stir until well coated. Using buttered spatula or wax paper, press mixture evenly in buttered 13 x 9-inch pan. Cut in 2-inch squares.

CREAMY PRALINES

2¼ cups sugar

1 (3 ounce) can evaporated milk

½ cup white corn syrup

¼ teaspoon baking soda

¼ cup (½ stick) butter

1 teaspoon vanilla

2 cups coarsely chopped pecans

In double boiler, combine sugar, evaporated milk, corn syrup and baking soda. Cook, stirring constantly, until balls form when dropped in cup of cold water or until it reaches soft-ball stage on candy thermometer. This will take about 15 minutes. Remove from heat. Add butter, vanilla and pecans and beat until it is cool and stiff enough to keep its shape when dropped on wax paper.

SNICKERDOODLES

½ cup (¼ stick) butter, softened

¾ cup sugar

1 egg

1 egg yolk

1⅔ cups flour

½ teaspoon baking soda

½ cup walnut pieces

½ cup raisins

½ teaspoon nutmeg

Sugar

Cinnamon

Preheat oven to 375°. Cream butter and sugar. Beat in whole egg and egg yolk. Sift flour and baking soda with nutmeg and mix into batter. Fold in walnuts and raisins. Drop from teaspoon 2 inches apart on buttered, cookie sheet. Sprinkle with sugar and cinnamon. Bake at 375° for 10 to 12 minutes.

WINTER WONDER DESSERT

28 chocolate cream-filled chocolate cookies,
    divided
2¾ cups milk
3 (3.4 ounce) packages instant pistachio
    pudding
1 (8 ounce) carton whipped topping

Crush the 28 cookies, reserving ⅔ of a cup. Place crushed cookies in a 9 x 13-inch dish. In mixing bowl, combine milk and instant pistachio pudding. Mix about 2 minutes until thickened. Pour over crushed cookies. Spread whipped topping over pistachio pudding. Sprinkle the reserved cookies over the top of the whipped topping and refrigerate overnight before serving.

COOKIES AND CREAM

25 Oreo cookies, crushed
½ gallon vanilla ice cream, softened
1 (5 ounce) can chocolate syrup
1 (12 ounce) carton whipped topping

Press crushed cookies in a 9 x 12-inch baking dish. Spread ice cream over the cookies. Pour syrup over the ice cream and top with the whipped topping. Freeze overnight. Slice into squares to serve.

EXTRA SPECIAL TREATS

CHOCOLATE SOUFFLES

With their crowns rising about 2 inches from the rim of baking cups, these individual souffles look very striking. Served warm from the oven, they just melt in your mouth.

5 (1 ounce) squares semi-sweet chocolate
5 tablespoons butter
½ cup sugar
2 eggs plus 2 egg yolks
½ cup flour

Preheat oven to 400°. Grease and flour 5 (6 ounce) ramekins. In top of double boiler or in small, heavy saucepan, melt chocolate in butter over low heat. Stir frequently until mixture is smooth and all chocolate melts. Remove from heat and cool to lukewarm. In separate bowl, combine sugar with eggs and egg yolks. Beat on high speed for about 6 minutes until mixture is very thick and falls in ribbons when beaters are lifted. Sprinkle flour over egg mixture and gently fold. Gradually add chocolate mixture and gently fold until all chocolate blends and mixture is evenly colored. Place prepared ramekins on baking sheet and fill with batter. Bake for 17 to 18 minutes until souffles puff on top. Serve immediately.

Tip: Although these should be served immediately after baking, they can be prepared in advance, put in baking dishes, covered and baked 20 minutes before serving. They may be chilled up to 1 day before baking.

APPLE DUMPLINGS

1½ cups firmly packed brown sugar, divided
¼ cup chopped pecans
2 tablespoons butter, softened
6 baking apples, cored
1 (9-inch) double pastry shell
½ cup water

Preheat oven to 425°. Mix ½ cup sugar, pecans and butter in bowl. Spoon into each apple. Roll half pastry to 1⅛-inch thickness. Cut into 3 squares approximately 7 inches.

Wrap 1 pastry square around each apple and pinch edges to seal. Place remaining 1 cup sugar and water in saucepan over medium heat and stir until sugar dissolves. Pour syrup over dumplings. Bake for 35 to 40 minutes or until tender, basting occasionally with syrup.

Tip: For even more flavorful dumplings, add 2 teaspoons cinnamon or apple pie spice along with sugar, pecans and butter.

BANANAS FOSTER

½ cup packed brown sugar

4 tablespoons butter

1 teaspoon cinnamon

4 bananas, sliced lengthwise

2 jiggers banana liqueur

1 tablespoon dark rum

1 jigger brandy

1 quart vanilla ice cream

Melt sugar and butter in skillet or chafing dish. Add cinnamon and bananas and pour liqueur and rum over bananas. Cook until fruit is soft. Add brandy and ignite. Pour over vanilla ice cream to serve.
Serves 4 to 6.

Tip: If you want a big flame, use 150-proof rum.

CHOCOLATE-COVERED STRAWBERRIES

2 to 3 pints fresh strawberries with stems

1 (12 ounce) package semi-sweet
  chocolate chips

2 tablespoons shortening

Make sure strawberries are clean and very dry. In small, heavy saucepan over low heat, melt chocolate chips and shortening, stirring constantly until mixture mixes and is smooth. Cool slightly. Hold strawberries by top and dip ⅔ of each strawberry into chocolate mixture. Allow excess chocolate to drip off strawberry into saucepan. Place on tray covered with wax paper. After all berries have been dipped, chill about 1 hour or until chocolate is set and firm. Remove from tray, cover and chill until ready to serve.